Seattle's International District:

The making of a pan-Asian American community

Doug Chin

International Examiner Press   Seattle, Washington

Distributed by the
University of Washington Press
PO Box 50096
Seattle, WA 98145-5096

ISBN 0-295-98197-0

B&T
4/02
14 95

Cover design and layout: Illustrations by the Design Team and layout by the International Examiner.

To my sons, Ryan and Daryl.

Table of Contents

Acknowledgments

Thanks to the King County Landmarks and Heritage Commission, King County Councilman Larry Gossett, and the City of Seattle Neighborhood Matching Grant for their help in funding the preparation and publication of this book. Had it not been for Holly Taylor, program coordinator with the King County's Landmarks and Heritage Program, this book would have not been written nor published. Holly encouraged us at the International Examiner to submit an application for grant funds to the Special Projects Program after we had been turned down for funding under another program she headed. She and Shireen Deboo, project manager with the City of Seattle's Department of Neighborhoods, were very understanding and helpful in the preparation of the manuscripts for this history book.

A good amount of credit and thanks goes to Melissa Lin, who did research and edited a couple of the draft manuscripts. Chong-Suk Han, the editor of the *International Examiner*, and Kalayann Domingo, likewise provided valuable research. Tamiko Nimura did copy editing.

A lot of thanks and appreciation goes to the following for reading and making invaluable comments and suggestions to the original manuscript: Sue Taoka, Bob Santos, Mayumi Tsutakawa, Gail Nomura, Richard Mar, Donnie Chin, Tama Tokuda, Cindy Domingo, Alan E. Yabui, and Gary Iwamoto.

Chong-Suk Han, Kris Proctor, Cahn Tieu and Tom Brierly all contributed to the design and layout of this book as well as overcoming all the information technology challenges in its preparation.

Further thanks goes to Eugene Tagawa for taking photos of the International District as it is today, and Ellen Suzuki for her excellent work in administering this project.

Last, but not certainly not the least, thanks to all of the board members of the *International Examiner* for their support: Aileen Balahadia, Nila Kim, Frank Irigon, Gary Iwamoto, Gene Kanamori, Arlene Oki, Connie So, Cindy Domingo, Pheobe Bock, Reed Harder and Andy Mizuki.

Financial assistance provided by: King County
Landmarks & Heritage Commission
Hotel/Motel Tax Fund

Forward

In the mid-1970s, I drifted out of college, a few credits short of a degree in journalism. I hungered to apply my newfound writing and editing skills in a real world setting. I went down to Chinatown to work for a budding young newspaper called the *International Examiner*.

To me, Chinatown was the logical place to go. It was my home turf. For as far back as my memory stretched, my family went there to buy groceries and attend family association banquets. For many years, my father waited on tables at the Hong Kong Restaurant, a bustling Chinese American establishment on the street level of a deteriorated hotel. I, myself, bussed dishes there on weekends and during the summer, from junior high school through college, earning money to support my education. My mother sewed at Seattle Glove Company, several blocks from the restaurant.

The 1970s was steeped in idealism and social upheaval. For me, the road from college brought me back to Chinatown to reconnect at a time when the neighborhood was sustaining profound change. A giant new sports stadium on the western shoulder of the area - the now-imploded Kingdome - had thrust the twin issues of development and preservation to center stage. Would this neighborhood, a cradle of Asian American history, survive? I wanted to see for myself.

From 1975 until 1987, I centered myself - with the exception of a few excursions into outside jobs that paid money - in the world of community journalism. I gathered news, edited, designed, pasted up and helped deliver the *International Examiner*. During that time, the paper chronicled the tumultuous evolution of the neighborhood, the transformation of Chinatown from a seemingly random assemblage of neglected buildings into a unified district where, block by block, individual projects began to take shape and illuminate a larger vision.

Student activists and returnees like myself began to call Chinatown another name, too, the International District. This conscious renaming was an attempt to promote a new identity for a community that has always served as home for residents, shopkeepers and workers of many nationalities. In this era, the assertive clamor of activists and elderly residents unleashed new public dollars to construct low-income housing, restore old hotels, establish bilingual social services and refurbish the streets.

In the early years, the *Examiner* was produced out of a dank little storefront on Eighth Avenue. We were all volunteers, college students mostly. We met and worked in a small front room lit by weak fluorescent lights, besieged by persistent water leaks dripping from apartments up above. We shared the office, typewriters and phones with the Alaska Cannery Workers Association, a group of young Filipino workers striving to uproot a longstanding tradition of racial discrimination in the Alaska canneries.

I spent many an adrenaline-charged night at the office preparing late-breaking news stories and editing feature pieces on International District history and history-makers. We always worked at full gallop. By today's standards, the Examiner's production methods were slow and crude. The stories were typed on manual typewriters, edited by pen, then retyped on a phototypesetting machine that spun out long strips of type for layout. In this pre-desktop publishing era, paste up was all done by hand.

In 1991, I left behind my journalistic career, joining the Wing Luke Asian Museum as its new executive director. I've been there ever since. With the comfort of a longer lead time, I now partner with others on developing exhibitions and programs on Asian American topics. Interestingly, I collaborate with some of the same people I worked with when I was at the *Examiner*. We're joined by a new generation of community enthusiasts.

What brought me to the Museum is what brought me to the *International Examiner*: the excitement of working in a community I care deeply about, a neighborhood in which threads of my personal history are woven throughout. Each thread unraveled - through inquiry and storytelling - reveals other connecting threads, entwined with the cherished memories and undiscovered family lore of other Asian Americans.

When my grandfather came in 1911 to this country from a small village in China - a village of Chews - he came directly to Seattle. Like other Chinese workers of his time, he lived in a claustrophobic little hotel room on Eighth Avenue and King Street, in the heart of Chinatown. Eighty-four years later, three generations later, my first son, Cian, was born into this community. Cian spent his first three years in an apartment just a block away from where my grandfather lived, in the core of what we now call the International District. In my family, the neighborhood - Chinatown, the International District - is what connects us, our four generations, all rooted in American soil.

I am grateful for the arrival of this book, *Seattle's International District: The Making of a Pan-Asian American Community* . For too long, what has been missing from our shelves is a readable history book that celebrates this neighborhood, a place unique on the U.S. mainland, a setting where, for nearly a hundred years, different Asian American groups have persevered to create a pan-Asian American presence.

This book is a collection of stories on the International District, written mostly by Doug Chin, and prepared under the auspices of the *International Examiner*. Doug researched and wrote the overview history. Doug and several other writers prepared the separate feature pieces. Melissa Lin assisted with editing.

Long-time readers of the *Examiner* will recognize some chapters and sidebar stories; they were published as sstand-alone articles, mostly in the 1970s and 80s, when the *Examiner* gave prominent billing to articles on local Asian American history. These pieces - repackaged together - provide a sweeping, yet pinpoint portrait of this pan-Asian community. They also spotlight organizations and individuals that have breathed personality and life into this neighborhood.

A few words about Doug. He and his brother Art wrote one of the first books on local Chinese American history: *Uphill: The Settlement and Diffusion of Chinese in Seattle, Washington* , published by Shorey Books in 1973. In the intervening years, Doug has authored many other articles on local history. Doug is easy to spot at community meetings: he is an unsparingly blunt proponent of Asian American causes and social justice. He always speaks his mind, mincing no words, deleting no expletives.

Doug served on the board of directors of the *Examiner*, on and off, from the time I first worked as editor - in the late 1970s - till last year. As an editor, it was great to have an activist board member like Doug, who took the initiative and time both to shame reluctant advertisers into buying ads and to write pithy articles on community topics. Doug's political savvy and his free-tongued advocacy, especially in the early lean years, enabled the newspaper to grow from a thin four-page tabloid into a publication which now has national reach and influence.

Congratulations, Doug. Congratulations, *International Examiner*. This publication extends your vital work into the book publishing arena. What a wonderful gift to our understanding of Asian American history that stories, which first found light in a favored local newspaper, can now find a more enduring spot in our book shelves at home and in places of research.

Ron Chew
Executive Director, Wing Luke Asian Museum

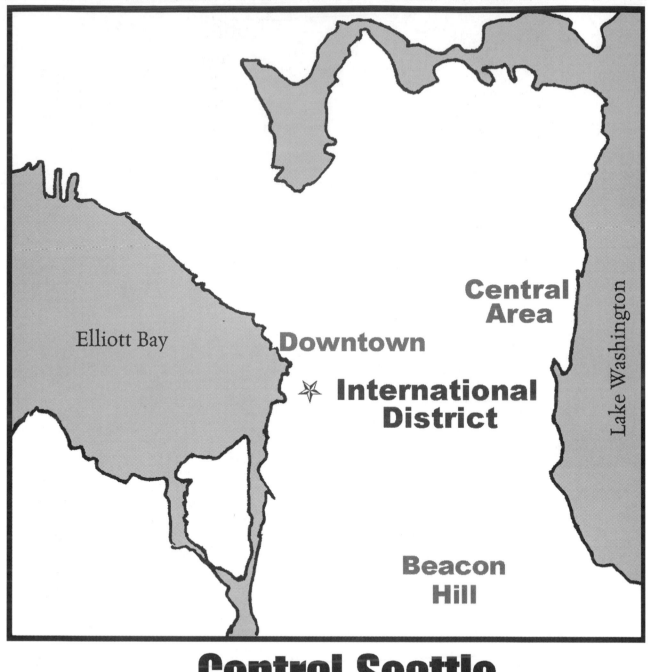

Elliott Bay

Downtown

Central Area

Lake Washington

★ International District

Beacon Hill

Central Seattle

International District, Seattle

Prologue:
The International District

South of Seattle's downtown business core, adjacent to the city's initial birthplace - Pioneer Square - and next to the train station, lies the International District. Also referred to as Chinatown, the District is a short walk to major league baseball at Safeco Field, as well as a new National Football League stadium. A growing 40-block downtown neighborhood, the District is the only pan-Asian American neighborhood on the United States mainland.

Established at the turn of the twentieth century, it is one of the oldest neighborhoods in the city. A major portion of the International District is on the National Register of Historic Places, primarily because it was the early settlement area for Chinese, Japanese, and Filipinos in Seattle.

It's more than fried rice, sushi, fortune cookies, cheap eats, chicken adobo, hum bows, herb stores, and a place to find ginseng that will make you young again.

It's more than Chinatown... more than a huge Japanese American supermarket...more than a place where you hear Asian languages and music...and more than an exotic locale for movie settings.

This is the community where different Asian immigrants settled, lived, worked and established businesses and institutions side by side. This is the area where the East met the West, where Asians collided among themselves and with the outside society.

The District was originally a very steep hill back when Seattle's early pioneers first settled there. That was way back when Holy Names Academy stood on top of Seventh Avenue and Jackson Street, its dome towering over the area. The school for girls originated there in 1884. That was in the very early days of Seattle when the tideflats reached Fifth and King Streets, and before the area was regraded, sliced to half its original elevation.

The days are long gone when the area was filled with hotels and boarding houses occupied by single immigrant men....when gambling, lotteries, opium dens, and night clubs ruled...when Japanese restaurants, bathhouses, pool halls and boarding houses crowded Main Street...when trolleys ran up and down Jackson and Yesler Streets...when the Japanese community flocked to the Nippon Kan to listen to the "red" and "white" teams debate the latest issue ...when crowds hurried to the only Chinese opera house in the area...when families grew bean sprouts in the basements of buildings...when open fruit and vegetables stands clustered the wooden sidewalks of Jackson Street....when jazz filled the night air...when Bruce Lee operated a kung-fu studio.

This is the neighborhood that gave birth to Asian American activism in the Northwest and the Asian American labor movement....where the country's first Asian American cannery union began...where a federal Supreme Court law case against Wards Cove canneries, which changed the course for national equal rights, was initiated...where the Japanese American Citizens League started...and where Japanese American Redress legislation got a boost...where people came to watch Chinese and Japanese movies...where the first Chinese women broke the traditional male dominance and became board members of the most powerful Chinese community organization and where a woman, Ruby Chow, ascended to presidency...where singer Ray Charles got his first contract to perform....where pan-Asian American community agencies, social services, planning, health networks and cultural institutions developed and flourished...where Asian immigrants come to find jobs...and where new immigrants start their business.

This was the home of Goon Dip, Chin Gee Hee, Ben Woo, James Sakamoto, Carlos Bulosan, Bob Santos, Donnie Chin, Chris Mensalves, Shigeko Uno and other community leaders....the setting for John Okada's No-No Boy, Peter Bacho's Dark Blue Suit, Monica Sone's Nisei Daughter...the location of the largest Asian supermarket and gift store in the Northwest...the social, cultural, and commercial center for Asian Americans in Washington State.

This is the most successful experiment in pan-Asian Americanism on the U.S. mainland, where the development of Asian American identity and character has made great strides. The International District is

Protest against the Kingdome. International Examiner file photo.

uniquely the only area in America where Chinese, Japanese and Filipinos settled and grew together, at most times cooperatively, with tolerance, but at other times much less so.

For much of its history, the District has been largely isolated, abandoned, neglected, and left on its own without much interest or assistance from City Hall or the rest of Seattle. The outside world just didn't care much about what happened or didn't happen in the area, as long as it did not disturb the workings of the rest of the city. The city's "tolerance policy" toward the area covered much more than crime.

Once the primary settlement area for different Asian immigrants and a refuge from the difficult and cruel outside world, the District grew from the interwoven stories of these different groups. Over the years, the area evolved as the regional center for Asian American culture in Washington State. The District is now the residential area in which Asian Americans remain the majority, and where Asian American commerce and culture predominate. Even with the new upscale development within and adjacent to the District, the area is where many new Asian immigrants still come to start their quest of the American dream.

This book traces the journey of early Asian immigrants to Seattle, describes their early settlements, and chronicles the evolution of the International District from its early times to the present. It covers the ebb and flow of the area, the struggles to preserve the area, the internal and external conflicts, and the important forces, government policies, events and people who have shaped the District. It is a story about the movement of the Chinatowns, the heydays of the 1920s, Filipino immigrants and union organizing, the internment of Japanese Americans, the decline of the District and how it fought back, and its emergence as a present-day pan-Asian American community.

University of California, Bancroft Library Collection.

Part One
Seattle's First Chinese Settlement

Early Chinese Immigration to Washington Territory

The emergence of Asians in Seattle and Washington State began with the Chinese. According to early records, Chinese in the Pacific Northwest first arrived in 1789 as part of Captain Mears' crew, which landed in Nootka Sound on Vancouver Island. No one knows what happened to them, but some speculate that they integrated with the native Indians. Other Chinese joined the crews of British ships that came to the Northwest along the Canton trade route, but those Chinese never settled here. The 1850 census showed one Chinese in Washington Territory: 19-year-old Ah-long, a servant to Captain Rufus Ingles at Vancouver Barracks in Clark County. There is no record of what happened to him.

Chinese came to America in larger numbers after gold was discovered in 1848 at John Sutter's sawmill in California. Circumstances at the time in both countries encouraged Chinese immigration to America. In 1842, China lost the Opium War to Great Britain. With defeat, China was unable to outlaw opium shipment into the country, and was forced to open its ports to trade with the West. Much of the countryside was in ruins, and peasants had to contend with ruthless landlords and famine. Heavy floods in the Pearl River Delta made conditions worse. The Taiping Rebellion, an unsuccessful peasant uprising in Southeast China, nearly uprooted China's imperial government. Widespread poverty, poor living conditions, and opression were reasons to venture outside of China. Meanwhile, gold fever spread across the Pacific Ocean, carried back to China by Chinese merchants from San Francisco. Soon, many journeyed to "Gold Mountain" - America - to seek their fortunes. Moreover, the demand for cheap labor on America's western frontier led capitalists and their agents to recruit workers directly from China to work in incipient industries, particularly the railroad.

Chinese immigrants to the continental United States came primarily from two provinces in southeast China: Guangdong and Fujian. Most were from seven districts in Guangdong: Namboi, Punyu and Shuntak (where people spoke the Sam Yup dialect) and Sunwai, Hoiping, Yanping and Toisan (where the Sze Yup dialect was spoken). All seven districts are on the Pearl River Delta south and west of Guangzhou. Many of the early immigrants came from villages in Toisan District. "Toisan" translates as "elevated mountain," an apt description of the area. For generations, peasants there struggled to eke out their existence from a harsh land. Two nearby seaports - Hong Kong and Guangzhou - attracted Western trade ships, which provided a ready means of travel for the Chinese sojourners.

San Francisco was the main port of entry for the Chinese in America. Although this city was to become the main Chinese American settlement, Chinese could be found throughout the West by 1870, particularly in California. They worked in a variety of occupations, including farming, railroad construction, mining, fishing and canning, and in the wool, cigar, textile, and shoemaking industries. Chinese men were also found doing domestic work - laundry, cooking, and house cleaning - because of the shortage of

Illustration by Steve Chin.

13

Chinese railroad workers. University of Washington Library, Special Collection.

women to do what was considered "women's work."

By 1870, there were 234 Chinese in Washington Territory, but only a few in Seattle. Most were in Eastern Washington seeking gold - following the trail of white miners from California and working their abandoned mines. With the depletion of gold in Eastern Washington, many headed west of the Cascades to Puget Sound to work on the railroad or in the coal mines, hop farms, lumber mills, fishing industry and other jobs. By 1873, there were 100 Chinese among Seattle's 2,000 inhabitants, and more arrived as Seattle's economy grew. Some came through Port Townsend, site of the U.S. customs house; others came via Port Gamble and Port Blakely, where they worked in the lumber mills. Some Chinese came to Seattle from points as far south as Portland and as far north as Canada. The first direct boat run between China and Seattle took

place in 1874. By 1876, the city's population reached 3,400, of which 250 were Chinese; an additional "floating" population of 300 transient Chinese laborers was contracted to various work sites outside Seattle.

Chinese Laborers in Washington

Largely because of Henry Villard, who financed railroads and their allied industries, Seattle's economy grew during the 1870s. Two of his major projects, the Northern Pacific Railroad and the Oregon Improvement Company, were instrumental in bringing the Chinese to Seattle. The Northern Pacific terminated at the nearby town of Tacoma and once employed 15,000 Chinese laborers, many of whom were shipped in from California. The Oregon Improvement Company exported soft coal and employed many Chinese in its mines around Seattle. The construction of the Seattle and Walla Walla Rail-

Steve Chin Illustration.

which had been grown at two gardens: one in the northern section of town on what is now the Seattle Center and the other along the Duwamish River, south of the city's commercial area. Some worked in factories, some did domestic work, and others found jobs in the lumber mills. Some worked on public works projects, clearing and grading many of the city's early streets; others engaged in net fishing in Elliott Bay. One Chinese even peddled ice cream from a converted wheelbarrow.

By 1880, more than 300,000 Chinese had come to the United States. Most were male sojourners who had come to America intending to make money, then return to their homeland (many European immigrants were also sojourners in this sense). In 1882, the year of the first Chinese Exclusion Act - which barred Chinese laborers from entering the U.S. - over half of those who had migrated to America returned to China, including a few who had made their expected fortune.

Steve Chin Illustration.

road, which Villard's firm eventually controlled, also employed many Chinese.

The Chinese, a reliable source of "cheap labor," attracted capitalist entrepreneurs interested in expanding (or venturing into) new businesses and others who demanded that the territory develop rapidly. At the same time, many Chinese sought work wherever possible, hoping to return quickly to their families and homeland. Chinese labor contractors based in Seattle contracted laborers out to various job locations within Puget Sound. Once their jobs were completed, most laborers headed for Seattle or Tacoma to find work there. Some of the more fortunate Chinese, who had accumulated enough money in the outlying areas, came to Seattle and eventually became successful labor contractors themselves.

The Chinese engaged in a variety of occupations within the city. Some worked in small businesses owned and operated by Chinese merchants. Whites and American Indians as well as Chinese patronized these small laundries, restaurants, and dry goods stores. The Indians, in fact, regularly patronized the dry goods stores and some Chinese employees learned Indian sign language and Siwash (the language of the local Indian tribe). Other Chinese peddled vegetables

Chinese Settlement in Pioneer Square

In 1860, there was still only one Chinese recorded in the census for Washington Territory. He was probably Chin Chun Hock, also on record as the first Chinese resident in Seattle.[1] Chin arrived in 1860 and began as a domestic worker - just nine years after the first white settler, Arthur Denny, landed at Alki Point.

The first Chinese to start a business in Seattle was Chen Chong, who began manufacturing cigars on Commercial Street (now First Avenue) in 1867. Chen was also the first person to establish a cigar business in Washington Territory. A year after Chen

Chin Chun Hock in center with cane. Wing Luke Asian Museum photo.

Chong, in 1868, Chin Chun Hock took his savings and opened a general merchandise store, known as the Wa Chong Company, next to the tideflats just south of Henry Yesler's lumber mill at the foot of Mill Street (now Yesler Way). The store advertised as a manufacturer of cigars and a dealer in sugar, tea, and Chinese goods. Some years later, the company advertised an added feature - opium.

Taking advantage of the need for workers and the growing Chinese population, Chin Chun Hock also became a labor contractor. His company additionally labeled itself as a "Chinese Intelligence Office" in its advertisements, asking anyone wanting to employ Chinese to contact him. The Wa Chong Company became, by far, the largest Chinese business in Seattle, and by the time he returned to China, Chin Chun Hock had become a wealthy and powerful person in the Chinese community.

Primarily a base for merchants until the mid-1870s, the Chinese quarter (in what is now Pioneer Square) developed into a commercial-residential area as increasing numbers of Chinese found work in the city. During this time, the Chinese quarters gradually shifted a few blocks from the Commercial-Mill Street area (what is now First Avenue and Yesler Way) to Washington Street between Second and Third Avenues. The new Chinese district was next to an area similar to San Francisco's infamous Barbary Coast, a rough-and-tumble Gold Rush neighborhood full of vice and crime. Chin Chun Hock led the shift by moving his prosperous Wa Chong Company to Third and Washington Street. Soon after, other Chinese merchants leased buildings along Washington Street from wealthy white property owners.

> The movement of Chinese into the area apparently caused such resentment in whites that property values fell and the city's business district grew in an unnatural direction.

The new location quickly became congested. "In 1877, Washington Street was Chinese Headquarters," wrote Clarence Bagley, a University of Washington history professor, in 1916. "On that street there were twenty-seven Chinese houses in about half of a block...During any alarm of fire they poured out like rats from a burning house".[2]

The movement of Chinese into the area apparently caused such resentment in whites that property values fell and the city's business district grew in an unnatural direction. "It instantly depreciated all surrounding property for business purposes," wrote J. Willis Sayres in 1936. "It is entirely likely that had it not been for those Chinese leases just at that time, business in Seattle would have followed the easier grades of lower Washington, Main and Jackson Streets, instead of going up the steep hill of First Avenue, which was a high bank on the east side and a drop off to the waterfront on the west side."[3]

In 1882, a school for Chinese children was established at the Methodist Episcopal Church at Fourth and Columbia; about 40 children attended. According to Bagley, the classes were taught by two white women: "The efforts of these two ladies and of the church to better the conditions of the Chinese and their customs were commended by the newspapers of that date."

Also in the 1880s, Chinese laborers dug the first canal connecting Lake Union with Lake Washington.[4] Work crews hired by the Wa Chong Company excavated and built locks on the log canals connecting Salmon Bay with Lake Union and Lake Union with Lake Washington. The two-year project, predecessor to the Lake Washington Ship Canal, was completed in 1885, just before the anti-Chinese riots which virtually wiped out Seattle's Chinese population.

Economic conditions grew worse in the early 1880s when a depression swept the country. As conditions worsened, antagonism toward the Chinese increased. By the time of the anti-Chinese riots in Seattle, in 1885-86, there were about 400 Chinese in the city, a small increase in 10 years. While the depression drove Chinese to Seattle, it also provided an excuse for whites to drive them out. The slow growth of the Chinese population (an increase in Seattle of only 1200 from 1800 to 1890) largely reflects the intensity of the anti-Chinese movement and the effects of the Chinese Exclusion Acts.

Anti-Chinese riots in Seattle, February 7, 1886, as depicted in *Harper's Magazine*.
University of Washington Library, Special Collection.

Part Two
The Anti-Chinese Movement in Washington

Anti-Chinese Agitation in Washington Territory

Antagonism toward the Chinese existed in Washington Territory even before they arrived in large numbers. When the territory was established in 1853, legislators immediately adopted a measure denying Chinese franchise. It is doubtful that there was even one Chinese in the territory that year, although there is record of one before then.

By the mid-1860s, after a scattering of Chinese began to make their appearance, territorial legislators passed more anti-Chinese laws. One law barred Chinese from providing evidence against whites in court cases; another measure was entitled, "An Act to Protect Free White Labor Against Competition with Chinese Coolie Labor and to Discourage the Immigration of Chinese in the Territory." The latter resulted in a "Chinese Police Tax," a poll tax levied against every Chinese residing in the territory.[1]

As in California, white settlers wanted to develop the territory for white Americans. Until the 1880s, however, overt hostility toward the Chinese was not always unanimous. In railroad construction, for example, whites generally accepted the employment of Chinese laborers. According to one historian, "the work was so obviously needed and all groups and areas vied with each other to entice a company to build a railroad in

their area that they would have welcomed the devil himself had he built a road...the lack of white labor was too evident to cause even the most ardent anti-Chinese to resent their employment on such work."[2] On some occasions, the arrival of shiploads of Chinese was greeted by cheering white Washingtonians. The importation of Chinese was a sign of economic prosperity and growth.

However, even when workers were needed, there was often enmity towards the Chinese. In 1874, when construction began on the Seattle-Walla Walla Railroad, some of its backers were so enthused that they "loaned" Chinese laborers to help build it. But whites ran the Chinese off the project and the sheriff had to be called in to protect the Chinese.[3] In Sultan (a small town northeast of Seattle), neither the whites nor the Indians, who perceived the Chinese as intruders, liked them. Eventually, the Chinese prospectors were run off their claims. On another occasion, a Chinese labor contractor had to write a letter protesting the mistreatment of Chinese laborers by whites at a lumber mill at Port Blakely. As a general rule, violence toward the Chinese increased as the number of Chinese grew.

By the mid-1870s, local newspapers and politicians frequently focused on the "Chinese Problem." The Daily Pacific Tribune, on December 27, 1877, referred to the Chinese as "money leapers" when commenting

on the departure of Chinese to Hong Kong. A Seattle newspaper, discussing the illegal entry of some Chinese, remarked, "If there is any cute trick in which Ah Sing is not equal of Brother Jonathan or any other man, it hasn't yet been put before the eyes of a curious public." On October 6, 1872, an article in the Snohomish Northern Star read:

We are glad to be able to chronicle one fact in relation to the Puget Sound fisheries. We are informed of the Tull & Co., formerly of Mukilteo, now of Seattle, after a careful trial they discharged all of their Chinamen and employed white men in their places. We are glad there is one firm operating our fisheries for the benefit of our own country instead of the Mongolian empire. There are hundreds of white men on this coast, who are knocking at our doors for work, yet "capital" brands them "tramps," casts them aside, and negotiates with some "Boss" of a Chinaman for a cargo of coolies to flood our land with this class of laborers, and grind the face of our poor still deeper in the dust. Shame.

With completion of the railroads and the onset of a depression in the early 1880s, the anti-Chinese movement in Seattle and the rest of Washington reached a crescendo. The Northern Pacific Railroad was completed in 1883, the Canadian Pacific two years later. Many Chinese who had been employed in railroad-building came to the larger cities in the territory to look for work - but in a

Anti-Chinese Riots in Seattle, 1885-1886. University of Washington Library, West Shore Collection.

depressed labor market, full of angry white workers also seeking work. Poor economic and social conditions led many to use the Chinese as scapegoats for rampant unemployment. Labeling them unfair labor competition and "tools of the Capitalist," Americans and European foreigners alike favored removal of Chinese from the territory. By 1884 the Knights of Labor had held many anti-Chinese meetings west of the Cascades. In 1885-1886, the anti-Chinese movement in Seattle - led by the Knights of Labor along with many prominent Seattleites - effectively resolved the "Chinese Problem."

Seattle's Anti-Chinese Riots, 1885-1886

The spark that precipitated the anti-Chinese outbreaks in Seattle was a riot on September 2, 1885, at Rock Springs, Wyoming. There, 28 Chinese were murdered and over 500 were driven out of town. Then, on the night of September 5, a group of whites and Indians armed with rifles ambushed a camp of 35 Chinese while they slept at a hop farm in Squak Valley (now Issaquah), a few miles east of Seattle. Three Chinese were injured and three killed. Five whites and two Indians were indicted, but they were acquitted after an eight-day trial.

Six days later, masked white men set fire to a building where Chinese workers lived in Newcastle, near the Coal Creek Mine. No one was hurt, but the building was destroyed, and 41 Chinese workers were driven from the area. At the Franklin Mines, another group of Chinese was expelled and their quarters burnt down. Members of the Knights of Labor led both attacks.[4]

In Seattle, the Chinese were no safer. Four days after the Squak Valley incident, the Seattle Post-Intelligencer reminded the public of the Chinese nuisance among them.

"The civilization of the Pacific Coast," the reporter remarked, "cannot be half Caucasian and half Mongolian." Of course, such a fear had no basis in fact since the Chinese were only a small percentage of the population. Also, Chinese immigration had all but ceased with the passage of the 1882 Chinese Exclusion Act: the first in a series of laws prohibiting the entry of Chinese laborers into the United States. Nevertheless, the Post-Intelligencer article exemplified the Sinophobia that prevailed at the time, confirming that racial and ethnic differences were just as significant as economic factors in anti-Chinese sentiment. Interestingly, just before the anti-Chinese riots in Seattle and Tacoma, nearly all of the Chinese were unemployed due to poor economic conditions or because the anti-Chinese forces had already driven them out of their jobs.

The anti-Chinese movement in Seattle consisted of two major forces. One group, known as the "anti-Chinese," favored direct action such as the forced removal of the Chinese in Rock Springs. The "anti-Chinese" were led by the Knights of Labor and were primarily working men, including European immigrants. The other main force was the "Law and Order" group, made up of prominent citizens and city officials. These "taxpayers and property owners" favored removal of the Chinese through legislative action. Their hostility was tempered by their concern for Washington Territory's reputation and chances of gaining statehood, and the fear of property damage that might result if violence broke out. Also, with an eye on the future of international trade, they harbored hopes that Seattle might become a "gateway to the Orient."

On September 28, 1885, the anti-Chinese group called the first of two meetings. At this meeting, the "Anti-Chinese Congress" resolved that the Chinese must leave Western Washington by November 1. On October 10, a committee formed at the September meeting invaded the Chinese quarters and warned the Chinese to leave. Then, on October 24, about 2,500 people participated in an anti-Chinese demonstration called by the anti-Chinese faction. Notified of the hostile situation in Seattle, F.A. Bee, the Chinese vice-consul in San Francisco, telegrammed territorial Governor Squire to inquire about his ability to protect the Chinese. Meanwhile, both the anti-Chinese and Law and Order factions agreed to meet with Chinese leaders. A meeting on November 4 with five Chinese labor bosses ended with an agreement for the Chinese to depart. The bosses only asked that the Chinese workers be permitted a reasonable amount of time to gather their belongings, dispose of property, and collect unpaid debts.[5]

On November 3, the day before the Seattle meeting, the loyal citizens of Tacoma loaded their 700 Chinese onto wagons and hauled them out to trains headed for Portland. Two days later, the citizens returned to burn down the Chinese quarters. The Tacoma incident heightened tensions in Seattle and bolstered the anti-Chinese group's belief that direct action was the best strategy for removing the Chinese. Frightened by events in Tacoma and the hostile atmosphere in Seattle, 150 Chinese left by boat and train over the next three days. Nevertheless, the situation remained hostile.

On November 8, 1885, the U.S. Secretary of War ordered federal troops to Seattle. The next day, 350 soldiers from Fort Vancouver arrived in Seattle with Governor Squire. However, from the actions of these troops, it is hard to tell that they were there to protect the Chinese. The uniformed visitors committed a number of brutal attacks on the "Orientals," of which six were formally reported. Four Chinese were beaten up in apparently unprovoked assaults; one had his queue cut off, and another was thrown into the bay. In addition, according to one reporter, a group of soldiers visited

University of Washington Library. West Shore Collection.

Steve Chin Illustration.

the Chinese quarters on the night of November 9 to collect a "special tax" from each "Oriental." This foray was supposed to have netted approximately $150. Discussing these outrages, the Call remarked: "The chances are that the people will be called on to protect the Chinese." On November 17, the troops returned to Fort Vancouver.

Over the next two months, people waited for legislative action to remove the Chinese and for the conspiracy trials of anti-Chinese group leaders. In an attempt to divide the anti-Chinese faction, 17 Seattle residents were charged with conspiring to deny the Chinese their legal rights. After 14 days of testimony, the jury deliberated for ten minutes and handed down a "not guilty" verdict. This decision, and the failure of the city council and territorial legislature to pass any effective measures disposing of the Chi-

nese, led to more hostility and strengthened the forces favoring direct action.

On Sunday, February 7, 1886, after a meeting of the anti-Chinese group the night before, a committee appointed at the meeting and their followers invaded the Chinese quarters, notifying the Chinese that they were to be sent away that afternoon on the steamer "Queen of the Pacific." Most of the 350 Chinese in Seattle were forced onto wagons and hauled to the dock. From that point, according to one historical account, "most of the Chinese were eager to get aboard and away from Seattle, but had no funds. The majority of them were in Seattle because they could not find employment in the mines or mills, had no money to move on, or were in debt to the local bosses for their passage to China and had no surety to save themselves".[6] Their departure was delayed one day by a writ of habeas corpus, sworn out by a Chinese merchant who alleged that his countrymen were unlawfully detained aboard the ship. Meanwhile, the anti-Chinese raised enough money to pay the fares of 188 Chinese, at seven dollars a head; eight Chinese managed to pay their fares themselves. Thus, on February 8, the ship left Seattle with 196 Chinese, the legal limit of passengers permitted aboard.

When the remaining Chinese were marched back to the Chinese quarters, shots were exchanged between the guards

and the crowd. One white man was killed and four were injured. The incident provoked Governor Squire to proclaim a state of insurrection, declare martial law, suspend the writ of habeas corpus, and request federal troops. At first his demand for troops was turned down on the grounds that troops could only be sent upon "last emergency." However, when prominent Seattle citizens became alarmed and sent telegrams to congressmen, President Cleveland sent troops. On February 10, eight companies of the 14th Infantry returned to Seattle. When the next steamer arrived on February 14, another 110 Chinese boarded. The remaining Chinese would leave on the next steamer.

On February 22, 1886, civil law was restored in Seattle, but federal troops did not leave until July. Only a handful of Chinese remained - a few laundrymen, cooks, servants, and bosses. Newspapers, labor leaders, and politicians sustained the anti-Chinese sentiment nevertheless. In the city and county elections of that year, the "People's Party," which had been established by the anti-Chinese group, made a clean sweep.

Aftermath of the Riots

A few years after the riots, slightly less than 300 Chinese remained among Seattle's 30,000 inhabitants. Economic conditions had begun to improve, helping to mellow anti-Chinese feelings. Chinese laborers were once again recruited to work at logging and sawmill operations, clearing and grading roads, domestic work, and railroad construction. In addition, some Chinese merchants tried to reestablish their businesses.

In other areas, however, the Chinese were still persecuted. One year after the Seattle riots, a group of 25 Chinese working near China Camp in Kittitas was attacked; all survived but one (7). The Chinese there had

> The sentiments of Washington's Senator Squire, the former territorial governor, echoed the feelings of many white Washingtonians and suggest that anti-Chinese agitation remained strong in the 1890s.

been recruited to work at placer mines after they had finished building the Cascade branch of the Northern Pacific Railroad. That same year, seven white men massacred 31 Chinese miners on the Snake River. Again, none of the whites were arrested.

Gradually, the Chinese began to drift back into the larger towns and cities in search of work. Gold mining had declined and few employers wanted to hire Chinese for work on the railroads or in the lumber mills. By 1890, there were 3,260 Chinese in Washington State, nearly the same number as before the anti-Chinese riots. Seattle had 359 Chinese, about half as many as in 1885. In Port Townsend, Spokane, and Walla Walla, separate Chinese quarters developed. Nearly two-thirds of all the Chinese in the state were located in these four cities. Tacoma, although it had had the largest Chinese population in the territory before the outbreaks, never reestablished a Chinese quarter, and the Chinese never returned to Tacoma in any substantial numbers because of the intense anti-Chinese hostility there.

Seattle's economy grew rapidly during the 1890s. After the fire of June 6, 1889, which destroyed most of Seattle's downtown, labor was needed for reconstruction. Publicity from the fire brought in more people and business, including what the city had fought hard for - the Northern Pacific Railroad. Yet when 40 Chinese arrived in Ballard (a district of Seattle) in 1892, the Seattle Press Times warned the public of "boat loads [of Chinese] coming." A man, described by the newspaper as an experienced employee of the custom house, cautioned: "These Chinamen...are of the class of fellows who usually get into this country. They are gamblers, convicts, and murderers. Fully one-third of these Chinese that come to this country have some sort of crime hanging over their heads. Chinese are safer in this country than elsewhere...There are a number of highbinders [Chinese] in this city."

The sentiments of Washington's Senator Squire, the former territorial governor, echoed the feelings of many white Washingtonians and suggest that anti-Chinese agitation remained strong in the 1890s. In a May 1892 speech before the U.S. Senate on the Geary Chinese Exclusion Act, he remarked:

...I ascertain from personal observation that a very large portion of the Chinese on the Pacific Coast are of a kind whose presence is deleterious to the best interest of society....I may be permitted to urge the view which is naturally taken by Americans of the Pacific Coast, that it is important to have the country settled by free American laborers who have respect for the institutions and laws of our country; who will establish permanent homes, and who will rear their families and train their children to have proper respect for labor even in its humblest sphere...the hiring of hordes of Chinese in the towns is thought to interfere with the healthy growth and development of society, and is a constant source of uneasiness and dissatisfaction to the white laborer.

University of Washington Library. West Shore Collection.

Buddhist church at Sixth and Main Street. Seattle Buddhist Temple archive photo.

Part Three: Nihonmachi (Japantown)

Early Japanese Immigration to Seattle

Japanese immigration to America began in 1868 with the restoration of the Emperor Meiji into power. For decades, under the Tokugawa regime's isolationist policy, Japanese were forbidden to emigrate to other countries; those who did so were not allowed to return. The first Japanese in America came to Hawaii, where there was demand for sugar plantation workers. In the first year of the Meiji Restoration, 145 Japanese, under labor contracts, landed in Hawaii without the consent of the Japanese government. Emigration to the island was curtailed for the next few years because the imperial government thought contract labor lowered the country's prestige. However, in 1886 the Japanese government legalized the shipment of contract labor to other countries. By 1896, over 22,000 Japanese workers had arrived in Hawaii. Robert Irvine, an American businessman who lived in Japan and acted as Consul General for Hawaii, arranged shipments of Japanese laborers.

The first Japanese workers in Hawaii came from areas around Tokyo, and their urban background apparently made it difficult to adjust to plantation work. Thereafter, workers were recruited from the rural areas of southwestern Japan - mainly from Hiroshima, Okayama and Yamaguchi prefectures. Most planned to come to America to save money and return. Poor economic conditions and political unrest in the early

years of Meiji rule provided an impetus to leave Japan, reinforced by the opportunity to make money in America. Demand for labor in the developing West was great, especially during the late 1800s. Workers were badly needed for railroad construction, lumber mills, farming, canneries and mining. The need for labor was especially acute with the curtailment of Chinese immigration resulting from the 1882 Chinese Exclusion Act. American companies eagerly recruited Japanese to fill the void.

In 1880, according to the U.S. Census, there were 148 Japanese on the mainland. Ten years later, there were 2,039. At the turn of the century, the number of Japanese on the mainland was 24,326 and had jumped to 72,157 by 1910. The two main ports of entry were San Francisco and Seattle. While many came directly from Japan, others migrated to the Puget Sound from Canada, Oregon, California, and Hawaii. The 1880 census listed one Japanese in Washington territory; he lived in Walla Walla. In 1890, there were about 360 Japanese in the state, the majority in Seattle. Over the next decade, the number of Japanese in Washington jumped to 5,617. This increase reflected the need for labor and the establishment of a direct steamship route between Yokohama and Seattle in 1896.

The first recorded Japanese in Seattle was Kyuhachi Nishii .[1] He came to America in 1884 from Kamiyama Village, Nishi Uwa-

gun, Ehime Prefecture, on the crew of a cargo boat that landed in Portland. Unable to secure a job after several months in Portland, he went to Port Blakely on Bainbridge Island to work at the sawmill. There were already some 20 or so Japanese working at the Port Blakely sawmill when Nishii arrived there, and perhaps a couple in Seattle.[2]

Seattle's Japanese Settlement Emerges

With a partner named Azuma, Nishii opened the Star Restaurant in Seattle on Occidental Street in 1888. It may have been the first Japanese business in Seattle, right next to the Chinese quarter at Second and Washington Street. Later, Nishii leased the Virginia Cafe with money he drew from a money pool with two other Japanese. He traveled back to Ehime Prefecture shortly thereafter and returned to Seattle with a bride and eight workers. Both restaurants proved to be very profitable and his fellow Japanese workers went on to open their own restaurants in Seattle, Bellingham, Tacoma and Spokane. Nishii eventually went to Tacoma where he partnered with others in new business investments and achieved continued success in the restaurant business. Nishii's restaurants, however, stood in contrast to most early Japanese businesses in the city.

A report by the Seattle Ministerial Federation noted that there were many Japanese-operated brothels in Seattle in the late 1880s, and a survey by the Japanese Consu-

Nippon Kan and Astor Hotel

From the time it was built until the internment of the local Japanese in World War II, the Nippon Kan was the heart of the Japanese community. The building was constructed in 1909 and located on the northwest corner of Washington Street and Seventh Avenue. The centerpiece was the theater, where local performers as well as performers from California and Japan put on traditional and contemporary plays, concerts, dances, puppet shows, martial arts, and variety shows. Japanese movies were also shown there. . Virtually all groups in the community used the hall—churches, business groups, sports associations, university students, and, of course, various cultural groups.

In addition, the hall was used for religious teachings and provided a forum for discussion of community and political issues. On many occasions, the "red" and "white" parties vigorously debated issues of Japanese politics on stage.

On the upper floors of the building was the Astor Hotel. The hotel offered inexpensive housing for new immigrants. Offices and meeting rooms were located at ground level.

The Nippon Kan's significance to the community was perhaps best demonstrated by [its control.] Ownership of the building initially belonged to the Cascade Corporation.[1] The corporation—estab-

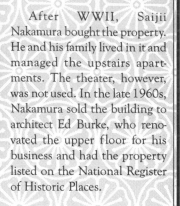

Nippon Kan Theatre. Wing Luke Asian Museum photo.

lished by Takahashi, Hirade and Tsukuno—sold shares to the Japanese community, which in turn supported it. Masajiro Furuya, head of the Furuya Company and its enterprises, later acquired the building. The Toyo Club controlled performances at the hall.

"A night out at the Nippon Kan was a welcome diversion from the rigors of work and school," wrote David Takami.[2] "Most of the entertainers were delightfully unprofessional, sometimes forgetting their lines and struggling to improvise. Between performances, children ran up and down the balcony staircases and their parents caught up on the latest community gossip."

One of the more notable performances held at the hall featured Shisui Miyashita, a famous composer and conductor. In 1936 he conducted the Seattle Symphony Orchestra, featuring pianist Sachiko Ochi, at the theater.

After WWII, Saijii Nakamura bought the property. He and his family lived in it and managed the upstairs apartments. The theater, however, was not used. In the late 1960s, Nakamura sold the building to architect Ed Burke, who renovated the upper floor for his business and had the property listed on the National Register of Historic Places.

In the early 1980s, Burke, who had taken on a co-property owner, completely renovated the property (including the theater) for commercial use, and added a penthouse on the rooftop for his own residence. Special care was taken to preserve the original features of the historic theater such as the rosette light fixtures, backstage graffiti, and an original curtain.

Now called the Kobe Terrace Park Building (after an adjacent city park of the same name), this elegant brick building stands at the highest point of the District, as if it was meant to symbolize the historic Asian American character of the area.

1. Ed and Betty Burke, "In a Chorus of Shadows: The Story of the Nippon Kan and its Restoration," in *Turning Shadows into Light*, p.47.
2. David Takami. *Executive Order 9066: Fifty Years Before And After*, Wing Luke Museum, 1992, p. 19.

Main Street. University of Washington Library, Special Collection.

Seattle was clearly the main settlement area for the Japanese in the Northwest as a new immigrant community emerged beginning on lower Main Street, from Second Avenue eastward, and on Washington, Jackson, King and Weller Streets from Fifth Avenue eastward. "If you should walk up Main Street from Second Avenue South, you will find where the Japanese town is," Kanada wrote. "It is safe to say that nearly all of the houses in this section are occupied by the Japanese." Included in his description of Japanese businesses were 45 restaurants, 20 barber shops, bathhouses, laundries, 30 hotels and lodging houses, four groceries, bakeries, meat and fish markets, five Japanese general merchandise stores, five tailors, two dentists, three physicians, four interpreters and some cigar stands and candy stores. The Japanese community had two daily newspapers and two monthly magazines. The North American Times was the evening paper and the *Asahi Shimbun* (The Rising Sun News) was the morning paper.

At the turn of the century, the ratio of men to women was 33 to 1. Japanese men in Washington were socially restricted from marrying the few white females available, and discouraged from returning to Japan because of travel costs and the possibility of being drafted into the military if they stayed longer than a month. Faced with these obstacles, many single immigrants resorted to arranged marriages. Through the so-called "picture bride" system, families or relatives would negotiate marriage on behalf of the groom through an exchange of pictures. The system was far from perfect; some men sent pictures of younger and more handsome friends, while others provided misleading information suggesting they were much wealthier than they actually were. It was not uncommon to find disappointed picture brides returning to Japan, finding another

late in the early 1890s found that the sparse Japanese population in Seattle was mostly engaged in illicit activities.[3] On July 1, 1891, Yoshiro Fujita - a secretary in the Japanese consulate in San Francisco - set out for Seattle under instructions "to make inquiries" about resident Japanese. After several months, Fujita reported that about 250 Japanese lived in Seattle, 40 of whom owned or were employed at 10 restaurants and one grocery store. To his dismay, Fujita discovered that the rest were gamblers, pimps, prostitutes or proprietors of brothels. Moreover, five or six of the restaurant owners, he reported, were connected with the prostitution business. "I can name only 10 individuals who have absolutely nothing to do with prostitution or gambling and indeed engaged in legitimate business or occupations in a strict sense," he wrote.[4]

However, according to another survey by

the Japanese government, conditions changed sharply at the turn of the century. The Japanese in Washington ranged from 15 to 35 years of age, wrote S.K. Kanada, a representative of the Japanese government, in a 1908 article in Washington Magazine. They represented not only the laboring classes, he said, but sons of samurai and a considerable number of college-educated men. Nearly all of this predominantly-male population made their living as waiters, domestic workers, shop workers, and laborers for the railroads, sawmills, and, later, canneries. Kanada identified four Japanese who had graduated from the University of Washington, two studying at that school and one attending Puget Sound University. He also noted that nearly 200 Japanese students were attending public schools and that the Seattle Japanese Association had established a private school for children.

man, or just escaping on their own. Men who could afford to return to Japan to find a spouse usually did so. However, a number of arranged marriages succeeded, and within two decades the male-female ratio had dropped to 2 to 1. The arrival of wives was of course critical to family formation, and was successful enough that the arrival of the second generation of Japanese in America was minimally delayed.

Christian churches were eager to recruit the new immigrants. The Baptists established a church for the Japanese in Seattle in 1899, with branches in Tacoma and Port Blakely, the site of one of the largest sawmills in the world. The Baptist church also had a mission for Japanese women, known as the Seattle Japanese Women's Home. The Methodist Episcopal Church established Japanese missions in Seattle and Spokane shortly after the turn of the century. Soon afterwards, the Seattle YMCA offered English classes for young Japanese. The Christian churches, in addition to providing religious teachings, served as social aid and educational institutions. They helped find jobs, providing English language training and counseling, and were thus instrumental in acculturating the immigrants.

Other institutions were founded by Japanese themselves and focused on retaining Japanese culture. In 1901, seven young men rented a house at 624 South Main Street and started the Seattle Buddhist Temple.[5] Seven years later, the Temple purchased land at 1020 South Main Street and constructed a new temple. It quickly became a lively community institution where picnics, Bon Odori (a street festival featuring traditional Japanese dances), and theatrical performances occurred. The Japanese Language School started on a small scale in 1902. It rented the second floor of the Furuya Company building and moved in 1910 to the basement of the Buddhist Church. In 1913, it completed a new building able to accommodate up to 1,000 students at 16th Avenue and Weller Street for $10,282. Hundreds of students attended the school's eight grades each day after public school for an hour and half, studying the Japanese language. The Japanese community was initially divided on the question of building a large language school.[6] Apparently, a good number thought that proficiency in the Japanese language was not necessary for American citizens while others, primarily the Issei, believed it was needed to retain and appreciate their ethnic heritage.

Elementary school students in the area attended Main Street School, at Sixth and Main. Miss Ada Mahon supervised the school. Nearly all of the 400 students enrolled were Japanese or Chinese. She later became the principal at the Bailey Gatzert School, which replaced the Main Street School.

Local Japanese Economy Develops

In its early stages, the economy of Seattle's Japanese section was primarily geared toward working men, with a large concentration of restaurants, barber shops, and hotels. The growing Japanese population - including those staying in the southern section of the city - consisted mostly of men who sought work on the railroads, in

Japanese Associations

Like other immigrant groups, the local Japanese community developed associations for social purposes, mutual aid, unity and protection. In 1900, the Japanese Association of Washington was formed in Seattle. Its first president was Tatsuya Arai.

Between 1910 and 1916, the Japanese Association was split into two camps, the Tobo Company and the Furuya Company, two firms that competed in supplying railroad workers and in the import of goods from Japan. Before long, however, anti-Japanese sentiment brought the factions back together.[1]

The first issue the Association addressed was the boycott of western-style Japanese restaurants, which they successfully resolved through mediation. It then split for a time and subsequently became the Japanese Association of North America. Until the 1930s, the Association was the main leader within the community. At its peak, the Association consisted of representatives of over 30 community organizations or clubs. It spent much of its time fighting discrimination against the Japanese.

In the 1930s, the Japanese American Citizens League emerged. A leading figure in the organization was James Sakamoto, also the editor and publisher of the *Japanese American Courier* newspaper.

Besides these associations, there were prefectural associations based on the locality from which the immigrants came. The largest among these was the Hiroshima Ken, followed by the Okayama and Yamaguchi prefectural associations.

1. Richard Berner, Seattle 1900-1920, Charles Press, 1991, p. 69.

Furuya Company

Among the Japanese businesses in Seattle, the largest were the M. Furuya Company and K. Hirada Company. Masajiro Furuya came to Seattle from Yokohama via Vancouver in 1890 at the age of 28. He was an educated person and an apprentice tailor. In 1892, after working six months in a grocery store in St. Louis, he opened a grocery at 303 Yesler Way, stocked mostly with Japanese goods.

The business prospered, catering to the large number of workingmen in the area and the growing Japanese population. In 1896, Furuya opened a branch in Yokohama. Shortly thereafter, he moved to a bigger location on Second Avenue South, and sold Japanese art products along with groceries. Later, he set up a post office in the store. Branches of the company were established in Tacoma, Portland, Vancouver, B.C., and Kobe, Japan. The company was also a substantial labor contractor, providing Japanese labor to the Milwaukee and Great Northern railroads.

In 1907, Furuya established the Japanese Commercial Bank. Seven years later, he acquired the Beikoko Toyo Ginko (Oriental American Bank), located at Fifth Avenue and Main Street. In 1923, he merged the Japanese Commercial Bank with the financially troubled Special Bank of Seattle. Five years later, the Japanese Commercial and the Oriental American Banks were consolidated as the Pacific Commercial Bank, with assets of $150,000. In June of that year, Furuya formed the Pacific Holding Company, with $960,000 in assets.

Furuya's enterprises were clearly the primary source of capital for Japanese American businesses and farms as well as a major employer. He became a millionaire, the only Japanese admitted to the Seattle Chamber of Commerce to that date; in July 1944, the *Town Crier*, a local daily newspaper, paid tribute to him.[1]

"Furuya was a hard-working boss who expected the same from his employees," wrote Susan Schwartz. "His clerks worked 10- to 12-hour days, their only vacations were when he let them visit his own resort at Crystal Springs on Bainbridge Island to picnic in the Japanese gardens he built there.[2]

In October 1932, the only Japanese financial institution went bankrupt. No one knows the precise reason for the downfall. Some said it fell victim to the Depression. Others said it was because of poor management, poor loans and bad investments. Regardless, the downfall of the bank meant the loss of substantial savings among the Japanese immigrant community, exacerbating the hardships brought about by the Depression.

1. Richard C. Berner, *Seattle 1900-1920: From Boomtown, Urban Turbulence to Restoration*. Charles Press: Seattle, 1991, p. 69
2. "The Rise and Fall of Japantown," *Seattle Times Sunday Magazine*, Feb. 8, 1976"

the timber industry, farming and fishing. Others sought work and fortunes in the gold mines of Alaska and the Yukon.

The first Japanese-managed hotel was the Cosmos House, which opened in 1896. Before 1900, there were three hotels and three rooming houses in Seattle operated by Japanese. They were inexpensive sleeping quarters, typically large rooms with up to seventy beds. Two were located on Washington Street and four on Jackson Street. The charge, including meals, was 45 to 75 cents per day. By 1907, there were 53 Japanese-run hotels in Seattle. In 1910, several operators came together to form the Japanese Hotel Operators Association and elected Chojiro Fujii as president. Fujii had come to Seattle at age 16 with his father, worked as a laborer, and in 1899 leased a small hotel at Fifth Avenue and Jackson Street and renamed it the Fujii Hotel. It quickly became the largest and best Japanese hotel in town.

Nearly all the Japanese-operated hotels were located around the Union Station. Most of the hotels were leased. Hotel management was by no means easy, but it provided a source of income and shelter for the managers and their families. The hotel business must have remained profitable for some time. World War I marked a period of prosperity and an increase in Japanese-operated hotels. In 1925, Japanese managed 127 hotels and apartment buildings in Seattle, totaling 8,575 units and employing 400 persons.

While Seattle was the headquarters for Japanese in Washington, their labor was needed to develop industries outside of the city. Thousands of Japanese were contracted to work in railroad construction, sawmills and canneries in the Northwest and Alaska. Seattle and Portland were the main centers for recruitment of railroad workers. At first,

Japanese Family. University of Washington Library photo collection.

Chinese labor contractors recruited Japanese workers. Later, Japanese contractors or subcontractors recruited directly. The first Japanese to recruit railroad workers was Tadashichi Tanaka in the early 1890s. An ex-sailor, Tanaka recruited 40 workers from Portland and sent them to the Union Pacific Railroad.[7] In Seattle, Tetsuo Takahashi began recruiting railroad workers in 1898, sending them to the Great Northern, Northern Pacific and other railroads.

One of the largest Japanese labor contractors in Seattle was the Tobo Company. One source mentions that the company solicited nearly 7,000 Japanese to work on the Great Northern, Northern Pacific and

local railroads. Even larger was the Oriental Trading Company of Seattle, which supplied some 15,000 Japanese railroad workers between 1898 and 1908.[8] The Furuya Company established a subsidiary called Furuya Construction Company and began to build the Oregon Short Line. Furuya and Tobo fiercely competed to recruit railroad workers in the early 1900s. Both companies paid $2 to solicitors for every worker they recruited. Furuya supplied workers to the Chicago-Milwaukee Railway and Northern Pacific. Typically, Japanese workers earned $1.15 for 10 hours of work per day, of which 10 cents went to the labor contractor. Whites received $1.45 per day.

Demand for labor in Northwest sawmills was especially critical. In 1907, the Immigration Commission reported that there were 2,685 Japanese working in the state's sawmills. The report mentioned that the Japanese, without exception, were paid lower wages than employees of any other race employed in the same occupation. Among the larger lumber mills where Japanese found employment were Mulkiteo, Enumclaw, Eatonville and Port Blakely. Evidently, the sawmills were the first industry in Washington to hire Japanese workers. According to the Japanese Consulate records, there were some 80 Japanese working at the sawmill at Port Blakely in 1891.[9] Very few worked as professionals.

Only a few Japanese worked in the fishing industry before 1900, but by 1904, some 1,721 Japanese were working in Alaska's canneries alone. Eight years later, they were firmly entrenched as a major non-white labor force in the canneries of Washington and Alaska, totaling 3,256. Numbers dropped dramatically as salmon production slowed during World War I; the number of Japanese cannery workers dropped to 611 in 1921. However, their numbers had risen again to 1,526 by 1928.[10] The Issei who went to the canneries of Alaska were called "Alaska boys"; many were migrant workers who worked in the California fields after the salmon season. They were scorned by the settled Japanese community.[11] Over time, many were replaced by students, who used the money they earned to pay for college.

In Seattle, Japanese cannery workers were first recruited by Tsuneyoshi Kikutake, who was subcontractor to Chinese labor contractor Goon Dip. In 1910 Kikuzo Ueminami was able to secure a primary contract, becoming the first Japanese labor contractor to provide work crews directly to canneries. Other Japanese labor contractors were Ichiro Saeki, Junichi Nagamatsu, Heitaro Obata, Tanejiro Kushi, Akira Taneda

Main Street School and Annex

The two-room Main Street School, which once stood at Sixth Avenue and Main Street, was known as South School when it was built in 1873. In 1889, students in the higher grades were sent to a new brick South School at 12th and Weller. In 1894, the Main Street building became home for the city's first kindergarten.

In 1903, the old schoolhouse was lifted and a second daylight floor with two classrooms was added below. Behind it, facing Sixth Avenue, a new annex was built.

By 1921, Main Street School had become the English-language tutor for the children of the International District. Only the annex on Sixth Avenue survived the construction of a two-story commercial building at the corner.

Main street school annex. Seattle Public Library photo.

and Tamizo Sakamoto. They sent thousands of cannery workers, Filipinos as well as Japanese, to canneries in Anacortes, Everett, Bellingham, Friday Harbor and Alaska.[12]

A 1917 survey by the Ministerial Federation illustrates the preponderance of Japanese working at small businesses in the service industry. Of the approximately 5,800 Japanese in the city, 85 worked for one of the three daily newspapers, 13 were employed in one of three banks, 27 were physicians, 17 were involved in religious work, 85 worked in notion stores, 33 were interpreters, 35 were druggists, 21 were midwives, 28

photographers, 28 worked in shoe repair shops, 100 were tailors, 150 laundry workers, 250 worked in hotels, 51 in pool halls, 56 in barber shops, 142 in American food restaurants, 170 in Japanese food restaurants, 221 in grocery stores, 38 in tobacco and fruit stands, 50 in clothing establishments, 86 in combined laundries, bath and barber shops, 19 in flower stands, and 17 in jewelry businesses. The report also said that some 2000 men and 700 women were employed as laborers.

Japanese Truck Farmers

Notwithstanding the importance of Japanese labor in the state's railroad, lumber and fishing industries, the Japanese presence in the development of local farming cannot be overemphasized. Japanese immigrants were well-versed in intensive cultivating farming methods. While they initially produced a variety of farm products, the Japanese eventually limited their efforts to producing vegetables, small fruits, greenhouse products and some dairy products.

The first Japanese-operated farm in Washington State began in the White River Valley in 1893. It did not take long for the industrious Japanese to begin farming in South Park, Georgetown, Green Lake, Vashon Island, Bainbridge Island, Bellevue and Puyallup. More often than not, the Japanese cleared and cultivated untouched land that they had leased. Much of the property was marshland which whites considered useless. Furthermore, most of the land farmed by the Japanese was leased or rented; state law prohibited land ownership by aliens (such as Japanese immigrants) who were ineligible for citizenship.

The White River Valley had the largest concentration of Japanese farmers. By 1925, some 65% of the Japanese farmers in the state were located there. According to the local Japanese Association, there were 231 Japanese farms in the area, covering 1,474 acres.

Most of the Japanese were engaged in truck farming. The goods they produced were regularly trucked to the city to be sold. These farmers supplied a number of produce stands and restaurants in what is now the International District. In 1907, five years after the Pike Place Market began, the Japanese started selling their produce there.

The Japanese presence at the Pike Place Market became a source of antagonism among some whites. Steps were taken to regulate the Japanese. One measure said that Japanese could sell only goods which they themselves grew, a restriction not imposed on others. Other measures attempted to take advantage of the Alien Land Law, which was passed by the state in 1921. Proponents argued that since Japanese did not own land, they did not have the right to lease space at the Market. Recognizing that there would be continuous attempts to limit their presence at the Market, the Japanese, in 1927, organized the Japanese Pike Place Market Corporation. The organization successfully fought back attempts to exclude the Japanese from the Market. Indeed, in the decade that followed, nearly 600 Japanese leased tables there.

By the time World War II began, the ambitious Japanese occupied nearly 70 percent of the Market. Pike Place Market became the place where many of the local Japanese farmers sold the bulk of their goods. Like other Japanese in the area, those who leased stalls were sent to internment camps during the war. Unfortunately, once the war ended the truck farmers never returned to the Pike Place Market.

Japanese farmers had also been productive; they played a key role in the development of the local agricultural industry. Their dairies supplied half of the city's milk supply in the 1920s. The Japanese also produced 75 percent of the region's vegetables and a good portion of the small fruits and berries. The gradual opening of an economic outlet for Japanese products, brought about by Japanese leadership, made possible an almost unlimited market for their produce.

In fact, the Japanese are credited with the expansion of the local farming market to the Midwest and Northeast.[1] Iceberg lettuce and peas were the principal crops. In 1930, some 2,230 carloads of lettuce were shipped by Washington growers, mainly the local Japanese. Moreover, Japanese farmers, accustomed to intensive farming, were able to cultivate crops like lettuce, peas, and berries on Vashon and Bainbridge Islands when whites were not.[2]

1.Ricard C, Berner, Seattle 1900-1920, Charles Press,1991,p.188.
2.John A. Rademaker, The Ecological Position of the Japanese Farmers in the State of Washington, Unpublished Ph.D. dissertation. University of Washington: 1939, p. 80).

Japanese farmers at Pike Place Market. Museum of History and Industry photo.

Chin Gee Hee Building at Second and Washington Street. Wing Luke Museum photo.

Part Four
From Sojourners to Settlers

Early Settlement in Old Chinatown

The local spokesperson for the Chinese in the 1890s was Chin Gee Hee, the most prominent Chinese businessman in Seattle. Well connected to Seattle's civic leaders, Chin operated a general merchandise store and was a very successful labor contractor. He watched the steady return of his countrymen to Seattle from his newly built Quong Tuck building at Second and Washington Street. The elegant structure was one of the first brick building constructed in Seattle after the Great Fire of 1889, which leveled the downtown area. Meanwhile, his former boss, Chin Chun Hock, constructed a building nearby on Second Avenue. The Second and Washington Street area also had three Chinese restaurants, eight laundries, a grocery and four general merchandise stores. These establishments formed the core of Seattle's early Chinatown. In addition, missionaries established the Chinese Baptist Church in 1896, in a rented building at Fifth Avenue and Yesler Way, which later relocated to Washington Street.

The 400 to 500 Chinese in the city lived in near-seclusion from other Seattleites, occupying rooms above the storefronts on Washington Street from Second to Fifth Avenues. After working long hours, they found respite in gambling and storytelling, and packed into these small rooms to sleep at the end of the day. It was mostly a bachelor society; roughly a third of the Chinese men were married, but most of their wives and families had stayed back in China. The Chinese found themselves competing for jobs with European immigrants, settlers from the Midwest and East Coast, and Japanese immigrants, who began arriving to work in sawmills and canneries throughout Western Washington. The Panic of 1893, which started four years of economic depression throughout the country, compounded the difficulty of finding work.

With the arrival of the Nippon Yusen Kaisha steamship line to Seattle in 1896, Chinese businesses experienced a modest surge in growth. The new steamship line not only provided direct passenger service to Asia, but also enabled Chinese businesses to get direct shipments from China. Chinese stores in Seattle began to stock their shelves with dried ducks, sweet-smelling roots, bamboo bales, herbs, smoked meat, tea and an assortment of packaged goods. The few Chinese merchants in town were now no longer at the mercy of Portland merchants. They became wholesale suppliers of Chinese goods to restaurants, general stores and work camps in the state and as far away as Alaska, Idaho and Montana.

Despite the Panic of 1893, Seattle witnessed one of its greatest periods of economic expansion during the 1890s - nearly doubling its population. However, the increase in the Chinese population only amounted to a single person. Chinese laborers simply were not in great demand. Although Chinese continued to arrive in the United States - in many cases, smuggled over the Canadian border - other Chinese left America for good, returning home to China. The situation looked so bleak that Chin Gee Hee, in an interview with a Seattle newspaper in 1899, predicted there would be no Chinese left in the city in 10 to 12 years. His prediction, of course, did not come true. Chin failed to take into account the enormous demand for seasonal laborers in the canneries on the Puget Sound and in Alaska.

Cannery Work Spurs Growth of Chinese Community

The Chinese had been a dominant force in the salmon cannery business since 1871, when a cannery operator began recruiting Chinese at the suggestion of his Chinese cook.[1] Thousands of Chinese worked the canneries along the Columbia River, where the Northwest cannery industry began. Chinese contractors recruited and hired the Chinese laborers, competing against one another for contracts. They were typically responsible for supervision, providing food, and paying crews at the end of the season, which lasted from April through September. The work was hard. Once the salmon were unloaded, the cannery workers gutted, cleaned, and prepared them for cans which were hammered into shape over iron cylinders. The cans were filled and soldered, and then cooked. The average pay was about $50 per month.

The first Alaskan cannery was established in 1878. Chinese were first employed as semi-skilled salmon butchers and cookers, and later replaced Alaska Natives on the rest of the canning processing line. By 1902, the Alaska cannery workforce of 12,431 included some 5,376 Chinese workers. Labor

Chin Gee Hee

Chin Gee Hee was born in 1844 and a teenager when he arrived in San Francisco. After a stint at laying railroad tracks, he came to the lumber mill at Port Gamble, Washington in 1862. There he washed clothes. In a few years, he sent for a wife from China, who became a cook at the mill.

A quick learner and a natural talker who was knowledgeable and conversant in current events, Chin became fluent in English as well as Samish. He developed many friends, including the family of Chief Sealth. At the urging of one-time Seattle mayor and lumber mill owner Henry Yesler, who frequently traveled to the Kitsap Peninsula, Chin and his wife moved to Seattle in 1873.

At the invitation of Chin Chun Hock, the owner of the Wa Chong Company, Chin Gee Hee became a junior partner by securing one-fourth of the business. Both men were from the same village in China - Look Choon village in Toishan.

Labor contracting became Chin Gee Hee's main interest and specialty. It was a job that perfectly complemented his language skills, bicultural knowledge, outgoing personality, and financial aspirations. He established the Wa Chong Company as the leading Chinese labor contractor in the Northwest Territory. He sent Chinese laborers to work on farms, railroads, coal

Chin Gee Hee. University of Washington Library, Special Collection.

mines, lumber mills, and public works projects, as well as to homes to work as servants or cooks.

The Wa Chong Company steadily grew and prospered with Chin Gee Hee's role as a labor contractor. Nevertheless, the company's involvement in labor contracting was troublesome to Chin Hock, who wanted the business to primarily focus on merchandise and dry goods, and importing/exporting goods to China.

During the anti-Chinese ordeal in Seattle, Chin Gee Hee was the leader and spokesman for the Chinese. He was quick to inform the Chinese Consul in San Francisco of events and the danger the Chinese faced. He also collaborated with Judge Thomas Burke to protect the Chinese, and represented the Chinese in talks and negotiations with the anti-Chinese committees. As a partner in the

Wa Chong Company, he and other Chinese merchants refused to leave until debts due to his company were collected, and maintained detailed accounts of riot damages, which he reported to the Chinese Consul. Chin Gee Hee was among those Chinese who were taken from the Chinese quarters and marched to the docks by the anti-Chinese mob. But with the help of Judge Burke and the city's business and political establishments, the well-connected Chin and his family were among the handful of Chinese who stayed in Seattle.

Eventually, the pressures of the anti-Chinese climate and the lingering business tension between Chin Gee Hee and Chin Chun Hock became too much to handle. In 1888, they agreed to go their separate ways.

One year later, Chin Gee Hee started the Quong Tuck Company, another general merchandise store that contracted labor and imported/exported goods. His new company occupied a storefront at the corner of Second and Washington in a new building that he had built. The building was one block from the Wa Chong Company and one of the first brick buildings constructed after the Great Seattle Fire of 1889.

Having achieved financial success, Chin could have returned with his family to China. Instead, he prolonged his stay. Because of Chin's connections with local political and business leaders such as Burke and Jacob Farth (a banker), Chin and his family were relatively safe, and he could continue doing business in the city. However, Chin hoped for the swift return of other Chinese to Seattle so that there would be a greater demand for his goods and services. But very few Chinese were in the city and so Chin recruited Japanese from Seattle and Chinese from Portland and San Francisco. These workers occupied his labor contracting jobs for the Great Northern Railroad and public works projects, including the cable car lines in downtown Seattle.

In 1905, he left the operation of his business to his son Chin Lem and son-in-law Woo Bing and returned to China to fulfill his dream of building a railroad in his native Toisan, the first railroad in China. Back in Toisan, he teamed with Yu Shek to form the Sunning Railroad Company. Between them, they raised $3 million to construct the 85-mile railroad from Toishan to Pak-Kat, which is near Kwongchow.

contractors from San Francisco, Portland and Seattle recruited the Chinese crews. The number of Chinese cannery workers making the seasonal trek to Alaska remained high until the 1910s and 20s, when it sharply declined to an annual rate of some 2,400 or about one-tenth of the total cannery workforce in Alaska.

At its peak in 1889, there were some 39 canneries on the Columbia River. Eventually, the salmon runs on the Columbia slowed and the number of canneries there decreased. Meanwhile, salmon canneries began sprouting up on Puget Sound at West Seattle, Mukilteo, Anacortes, Bellingham, Blaine, and Port Blakely. In a few years, the fishing industry became one of the state's most prosperous enterprises, generating revenues in excess of $5.5 million. As the canneries grew along Puget Sound, the Chinese were hired in greater numbers. Over 2,000 arrived annually by boat, hundreds at a time, from Portland and San Francisco. On Bellingham Bay, as elsewhere, a "China House" was built with a kitchen, dining room, storeroom, store and living quarters for 200 Chinese.

At the end of the cannery season, more and more of the men chose to go to Seattle, where they found housing more plentiful and cheaper than in Portland or San Francisco. Almost overnight, more Chinese businesses appeared. Chinatown grew to three blocks on Washington Street and two side streets. Stores were located at the street level and rooms for lodging on the upper levels. The Wa Chong Company, Quong Tuck Company, and Mark Ten Suie - the "big three" - were the largest, oldest and most prosperous Chinese businesses at the turn of the century. The cannery business benefited Chinese labor contractors in other ways, as it provided housing, food and other services to the laborers at a cost, often extending them credit when they were not working. In

addition to the big three, Chinatown was the site of the Hop Sing Tong "joss house" and over 20 other businesses, including tailor shops and curio shops that catered exclusively to Americans. Seattle began to replace Portland as the largest Chinese settlement in the Northwest.

In 1902, the "Iron Chink" appeared, a complicated machine that was supposed to butcher the fish and eventually replace the Chinese workers. The "Iron Chink" did mechanize some tasks, but it didn't get rid of the Chinese. Workers were still needed to operate the machines. Cannery labor contractors like Chin Gee Hee, Woo Gen of the Wa Chong Company, Mark Ten Suie and later Mar Dong, Chin Seay, Goon Dip (and others) were able to make huge profits while dominating cannery worker recruitment. The workforce also included Japanese and Filipinos. The canneries remained a major source of employment for Chinese until the 1930s, when a union supplanted the Chinese contractors. Contracted Chinese laborers also helped complete the Northern Pacific Railroad to Seattle, constructed buildings, paved streets, and worked on other public works projects.

Despite the economic growth in Seattle and the state during the 1890s, the Chinese population increased very little. Census figures for 1900 showed 438 Chinese in Seattle and 3,629 in the entire state, widely dispersed throughout Washington with the largest concentration in Whatcom County, where they worked in the canneries. At the close of the first decade of the 1900s, the number of Chinese working on jobs outside Seattle - other than in the fishing industry - had declined considerably. Most Chinese in the state were employed in the fishing industry during this period. Thousands of Chinese worked in these canneries - hooking, cleaning, and packing fish - as late as the 1930s.

Development at Second and Washington

The Chinatown at Second Avenue and Washington Street slowly developed as Chinese came from other parts of Washington; demand for Chinese labor in those areas had ceased. Most Chinese businesses in Chinatown were general merchandise stores that sold imported Chinese products and American goods (surprisingly, few Chinese laundries and restaurants flourished at the turn of the century). The largest stores were the Quong Tuck Company, owned by Chin Gee Hee; Ah King Company (also known as King Chong Lung Company) owned by Eng Ah King; and the Wa Chong Company owned by Chin Chun Hock. All three storeowners were also labor contractors or agents who contracted Chinese to work on railroads and farms, and in lumber mills and canneries; all three became wealthy from the growth of the Chinese community.

In 1905, Chin Gee Hee left the operation of his business to his son Chin Lem and son-in-law Woo Bing and returned to China to fulfill his dream of building a railroad in his native Toisan.

That same year, the Chinese Imperial Commission passed through Seattle on its way to Europe. The City put on its best face in an effort to lure the China market. "Seattle looks to the Orient for much of her future greatness," a newspaper reporter wrote. "Chinese can consume our ware in ever increasing measure; China can take our steel, our foodstuff...Upon the potent power that China someday may hold in the palm of her hand depends much of Seattle's prosperity." Ironically, just 20 years earlier, Seattle citizens, abetted by the media, had tried to expel the Chinese, who had done more than any other group of people to establish and promote trade between China and Seattle. Since their arrival in the 1860s, Seattle's Chinese merchants had been involved in the import and export of goods between Seattle and China.

"The Chinese population of the city of Seattle can truthfully be classified as among the pioneer builders of the great Pacific Northwest," wrote Lew G. Kay, the first Chinese to graduate from the University of Washington, in a 1909 article in Coast Magazine:

"Some of them have returned to their fatherland to assist in the industrial and commercial revolution which will greatly increase the trade in the Orient and thus to make the Pacific Ocean as the main channel of the world's commerce...The local Chinese community, although small in number, has ever been ready and willing to assist in advancing the interest of the Pacific Northwest in the struggle for commercial supremacy in the distant Orient. This was recently exemplified by the placing of large shipments of modern machinery to local firms, through the influence of former Chinese merchants of Seattle who have returned to China as financial and industrial leaders."

Chinese School

One of the oldest Chinese institutions in Seattle is the Chinese school. Nothing was more important to the Chinese than teaching Chinese language and culture to the young. In the early 1900s, the curriculum included Chinese history, the teachings of Confucius, and Chinese language. Children from 5 to 18 years old attended Chinese school five days a week after public school and on Saturdays. Chinese school was also held through the summer.

Chin Chun Hock — and later, Goon Dip — paid most of the operating expenses of Seattle's Chinese school. Parents of students also covered part of the expenses.

For a short period before the overthrow of the Manchu Dynasty, the Chinese imperial government even arranged for teachers to come over from China and matched the school funds raised by local merchants.

School was held on the first floor of a two-story building at 12th and Yesler Way, the same site as the Honorary Chinese Consulate's office. Eventually, the school was supported through funds raised by the Chong Wa Benevolent Association, the major umbrella organization of the Chinese family associations and tongs in Washington state.

The school had no more than 15 students when it began around the turn of the century. In 1909, that number increased to 42, after a Chinese woman editor from San Francisco chastised school trustees for not allowing girls to attend. Even though the school changed its restrictive policy by allowing females, enrollment did not increase substantially.

In 1930, when the school relocated to the newly built Chong Wa Benevolent Association building, enrollment reached 100 and peaked at 275 during World War II. The small size of Chinese school enrollment at that time reflected the small number of Chinese families in the city. There were only a handful of families in 1900 and the number increased only slightly until the 1940s.

Lew Kay's article appeared in the same year as the Alaska-Yukon-Pacific Exhibition, a world's fair held at the University of Washington campus. Goon Dip, formerly of Portland, arrived in Seattle in 1908 to organize efforts to create a Chinese pavilion for the Exhibition. Goon had previously been appointed the Honorary Chinese Consul for the Northwest, beating out Chin Gee Hee; he was one of the labor contractors who sent Chinese to the canneries of Bellingham and, later, to Alaska. Another Chinese contractor, Ah King, president of the King Chong Lung Company, helped finance the pavilion; nearly every Chinese in the city contributed $4 to the undertaking.

Coincidentally, in 1909, Seattle was completing work on the Jackson Street Regrade Project: a major engineering project which involved filling in Jackson and King Streets with dirt, converting land that had been covered with tidal flats into an area for development. The timing of the project was perfect for the Chinese, whose numbers had doubled to 900 in the last decade. Washington Street was becoming too congested. The International Chinese Business Directory of the World for 1913, which was published in San Francisco and always contained data that was at least two years behind, listed 41 businesses in Seattle's Chinatown. These included 28 general merchandising stores, two laundries, three associations, two restaurants, two Chinese and Japanese bazaars, two ladies' underwear shops, a drugstore, and a bird and goldfish store. After completion of the regrade project, Chinese expanded their settlement into what was to become present-day Chinatown.

Second and Washington Street. Seattle Public Library photo.

Chinatown Shifts to King Street Core

The Chinese began occupying lower King Street immediately after completion of the Jackson Street Regrade Project. The first Chinese buildings constructed in the King Street core were the Hip Sing Tong building on the northwest corner of Eighth and King Street and two huge buildings between Seventh and Eighth Avenues South on the south side, built in 1910. A Chinese group, the Kong Yick Investment Company headed by Goon Dip, was established for the sole purpose of constructing the latter two buildings. Shares were sold to Chinese throughout the Northwest to finance the projects. (No bank financing was involved; Chinese at that time ignored banks, and vice versa.) The Wa Chong and Quong Tuck Companies immediately moved to the Kong Yick buildings. Also setting up shop there were the Yuen Long Company and Yick Fung Company, an importer/exporter and agent for the Blue Funnel steamship line. These were the first Chinese businesses on King Street. One of the Kong Yick buildings later housed the Gee How Oak Tin Family Association, the largest Chinese family association in the state, and the elaborate King Fur Cafe.

The following year, 1911, Goon Dip built the Milwaukee Hotel, an elegant structure on Seventh and King Street. The top floor of the hotel served as his family's residence.

The District before the Jackson Street Regrade. Seattle Public Library photo.

The Jackson Street Regrade

Over 65 years ago, much of what is now the International District or Chinatown was once covered with tideflats. Elliott Bay came up to what is now Fifth Avenue and South Jackson Street. The tideflats went up to Fifth Avenue and Lane Street, and curved around old Beach Road to the foot of Beacon Hill. (Note: Jackson Street was partially regraded in 1883 between Tenth and Twelfth Avenues.[1]

Then, in 1907, the city decided to regrade Jackson Street. The shoreline was stretched outward into the bay as the tideflats were filled.

Above what was Eighth Avenue before the regrade, was a very steep hill. On the southeast corner of Ninth and Jackson stood Holy Names Academy. The Academy was moved because of the regrade project.

The top of the hill, along 12th Avenue,

was nearly as high as the top of Beacon Hill with only a small slope at Dearborn Avenue (presently the Jose Rizal Bridge) connecting the two hills.

The terrain made it difficult for farmers in Rainier Valley to bring their produce to downtown markets. Some farmers had to go around Auburn to get to town.

R.H. Thomson, city engineer at the time, considered building a tunnel through Beacon Hill. He chose to regrade Jackson instead because it was less expensive and would benefit the area more than the tunnel project.

There were 62 regrades in the city. The Jackson Street Regrade was the largest at the time. It extended all the way south to Lander Street and westward to Alaskan Way.

The proposed plan called for a 90-foot cut at Ninth and Jackson, where the freeway now stands. According to Bill Spiedel, former editor of the *Seattle Guide*, "you can put an eight-story building on top of the freeway...that was how high the hill was."

In 1907, the Lewis and Wiley Company was contracted for the project. A young civil engineer, W.C. Morse, informed Lewis, and Eastern-trained lawyer and property owner in Rainier Valley, of the hydraulic method of regrading. He advised Lewis to begin an excavating company. Lewis did so – under Morse's supervision.

Shortly after the Jackson regrade began, the city also decided to regrade Dearborn Street slope and to replace it with a bridge to connect Beacon Hill with Jackson Street, which they did.

The entire project was a gigantic undertaking. According to a report by the Seattle Engineering Department, five and three-quarter miles of street or 56 city blocks were involved in the project.

"The greatest cut was 85 feet at Ninth Avenue and Jackson Street; the grade of Jackson Street was reduced from 15.16 percent to 5.04 percent; and the street was widened from 66 feet to 96 feet. Grades on the streets to the north of Jackson were left steep, but to the south they were brought down to 7.25 percent at the maximum on Weller Street and correspondingly on the other streets."

The hill was composed mostly of hard blue clay with little rock formation. The clay would shatter with only light blasting. A method called "sluicing," using a water hose with added air pressure from a pipe connected to the nozzle, was used.

Water for the sluicing first came from Jefferson Park Reservoir. Later, pumping stations on Lake Washington and at the foot of Connecticut Street were added. The sluicing operation was carried to within a foot of the finished grade, the report said. The final grading was done with "horse-drawn scraper."

The pumps used on the sluicing operation were like those used on the Denny Regrade, the largest resurfacing project in the city. The pump operators were veterans from Alaskan hydraulic mining operations.

"The process of mixing water and earth and various soils, and keeping the face of the excavation and the pipe line open and full to capacity," the report said, "was an interesting sight that brought full galleries of 'sidewalk superintendents.'"

The project, understandably, was not without problems. Sanitation in the District worsened with the filling of the tideflats because the drains and sewers got plugged. In addition, "many of the buildings rested almost on the ground and had flooded during high tides," the report said. "Some were raised on blocks and filled underneath."

The regrade also created problems for some Japanese merchants on Main Street. According to a 1909 article in Coast Magazine by the Japanese Consulate in Seattle, some of the merchants had to move their businesses down to Weller Street.

The entire Jackson regrade project was completed in 1914.

1. Paul Dorpat, *Seattle Times*, October 17, 1999.

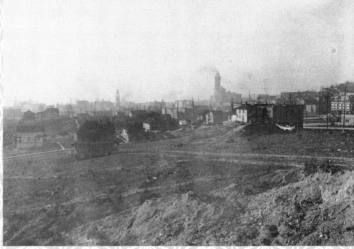

The District after the Jackson Street Regrade. International Examiner file photo.

Margaret Chin

Among the small number of women in the community, there is no greater story of strength and courage than that of Dong Oy and her daughter, Margaret Chin. Dong Oy was the wife of Chin Gee Hee's son, Chin Lem.

Chin Gee Hee, concerned that his son had had a daughter rather than a son as heir to his fortune, ordered Chin Lem, Dong Oy, and their daughter back to Sunning (the former name of Toisan). There, Chin Lem deserted his wife and went off to find a new wife as Chin Gee Hee had insisted. After a year, Dong Oy fled to Hong Kong with her daughter, arriving at her mother's house.

Afraid that the mother and daughter would leave for America, Chin Lem sought them out. He bought a 2-month-old boy and told Dong Oy to go to authorities and get a birth certificate to document the baby as their son. Then, he said, they could all leave for Seattle. But after she obtained the birth certificate, Chin Lem said he had no money. Dong Oy withdrew $700 of the $900 she had at a Shanghai bank and gave it to Chin Lem to purchase tickets. But he disappeared with the money.

For months, Dong Oy searched for her estranged husband to no avail. In desperation, she pawned her jewelry to get herself and her daughter to Seattle. That afternoon police officers came to the home of relatives, where she was staying, and issued a warrant for falsely swearing to the boy's birth certificate. When she appeared in court, there was Chin Gee Hee, along with his relatives.

Dong Oy's mother, with help from her friends, raised $250 bail for her daughter's release. However, Chin Lem was able to convince Dong Oy to jump bail and return to Sunning, which she did. There, her husband deserted her for the last time.

Courageously, Dong Oy and fled with Margaret to another village, where she disguised herself as an old lady and Margaret as a young woman. Although Chin Gee Hee had ordered surveillance for all seaports and railroad stations, they were able to evade guards and reach Hong Kong. After two months in hiding, they took a steamer to Shanghai and then Yokohama, where Dong Oy sold the last of her jewelry (worth $80) for passage on the *Empress of India*. They arrived in Seattle in April 1909, when Margaret was 12 years old.

In Chinatown, Dong Oy took care of babies and sewed to earn a living. In 1917, while Margaret was in her second year at the University of Washington, they started a Chinese tea room named Sunning at Fourteenth Avenue Northeast (now known as University Way or "the Ave") in the University District. Admiration and respect for Dong Oy increased within the community, as well as among her many white friends.

Margaret later married Sam Chin, the first Chinese licensed architect in the state and the designer of the Chong Wa building. Despite his education and training, Chin never really worked as an architect; racial discrimination prevented most Chinese American college graduates from finding employment in their chosen professions.

That same year, the Eastern Hotel building was built on Maynard Avenue between King and Weller Streets, supposedly for the Wa Chong Company. In 1916, the Bing Kung Tong constructed a building on King Street across from the Kong Yick buildings and, in 1920, the Chew Lin Association built the Republic Hotel building on Seventh Avenue South between Jackson and King Streets. Other Chinese either built or purchased other buildings along King Street. Of the dozen or so Chinese restaurants in Seattle in the late 1910s, about half were located in what is now the International District and the rest in the old Chinese quarters on Main Street or downtown. Interestingly, most of the 30 or so Chinese hand laundries at the time were located outside of the new or old Chinatown areas.

By 1925, King Street had become the core of the main Chinatown in Seattle. The old Chinatown on Washington Street had withered away to little more than a bunch of lottery and gambling houses. The new Chinatown on King Street was only a few blocks southeast of the old Chinatown and right next to the Japanese settlement, which extended from Second to Twelfth Avenue, between Yesler Way and Jackson Street. There were also a good number of Italian and African American establishments throughout the area and, later, Filipino businesses. Rainier Heat and Power Company, which owned seven or eight large pieces of property, was by far the largest single property owner in the area.

One of the earliest outside visitors to the new Chinatown was Dr. Sun Yat-Sen, who led the overthrow of the Manchu Dynasty in China. Sun, the founder and first president of the Republic of China, arrived in Seattle in September 1911, just one month before the Manchus were overthrown. Sun had garnered great support from the overseas Chinese, who contributed generously to his revolutionary movement. One hundred and fifty people attended Sun's fundraising event, supposedly shrouded in secrecy. Dinner was held at the King Fur Cafe, on the second floor of the newly built Kong Yick building. After dinner, Dr. Sun gave a one-hour speech on the third floor, the temporary location of the Gee How Oak Tin Family Association. He told a 13-year-old boy after his talk: "There are 400 million people in China, but if I had just one million like you, I know we would have a successful revolution and, perhaps, a united China."

A Single Man's Society

The Chinese community in Seattle was a small, isolated community. It was essentially composed of aging single men who were, for the most part, more like immigrants in their orientation than sojourners. They had lived most of their lives in America, and only thought of returning to China in their old age to live out their remaining years.

In 1910, the median age of Chinese in Washington State was 45. Ten years later, it was 42. The median age of Chinese in Seattle could not have been much different. It was clearly a community of mostly older men who had come to Seattle for work. Many had been in the States for a long time, but had yet to achieve enough wealth to return. Others, despite the hardships, felt that opportunities and living conditions were better in America than the villages from which they came.

In 1910, there were 860 males and 72 females - a ratio of 13 to 1. Ten years later, there were 1,180 males and 181 females. In 1930, there were 1,000 males to 350 females and, in 1940, 1,350 males to 450 females. Not until the 1970 census did the ratio of males to females come close to being proportional. Clearly, the 1882 Chinese Exclusion Act and subsequent exclusionary acts had severely impeded the growth of families; these acts made it virtually impossible for Chinese women other than wives of merchants and other members of exempt classes to enter the United States. Single Chinese men could have married outside of their race as sojourning Chinese did in other countries. However, while there was no state law prohibiting miscegenation, social norms of the white society precluded such a possibility. "You know Chinese no allowed to marry white girl in California and Oregon," Woo Gen, one of the partners in the Wa Chong Company, said. "Only in Washington and up here make lots of trouble."[2] It would take decades before the critical mass for a second generation would emerge.

By 1920, migration of Chinese to Seattle from other parts of the Northwest, mainly Portland, had all but ceased. Legal immigration from China, of course, ended with the passage of the 1882 Exclusion Act. However, the Chinese continued to come to America through two methods: first, by claiming that they were merchants, a group exempt from

the exclusion laws. To earn that status, they bought partnerships in Chinese American businesses; these businesses frequently had a large number of partners, only a few of whom actually ran the business.

Second, and perhaps more significantly, many immigrants falsely claimed American citizenship. After a 1906 San Francisco fire destroyed city records, Chinese began claiming to have been born in America - making them automatic citizens. No one could challenge them. If these "American-born citizens" returned home to China, they invariably reported the birth of sons. Years later, when these sons - some real and some "paper son" impostors - came of age, they were permitted by birthright to join their fathers in America.

Except for seasonal work in the canneries of Alaska and Bellingham, outside work in the white society was almost non-existent for these bachelors. They were hamstrung by their inability to speak English, their lack of skills and education, and anti-Chinese discrimination. Typically, they worked long hours at Chinese restaurants, import/export stores, general merchandise stores, curio shops, hotels, gambling houses, or in the canneries. And, they usually had to join one of the tongs - secret societies that controlled most of the gambling and lottery houses and assisted its members with jobs and protection. Others worked at hand laundries; in 1920, there were over 30 Chinese hand laundries in the city, most located in the downtown area outside of Chinatown, with several on Capitol Hill. The bachelors lived in cramped rooms in Chinatown hotels, tong buildings or family associations. The merchant families, of which there were few, lived in hotel units that combined single rooms. Leisure time was a relatively unknown commodity; children would play in the alleys or vacant lots, seldom roaming outside of Chinatown except for school.

Wing Luke Asian Museum photo.

Part Five
Filipinos Arrive in the District

Early Filipino Immigration to Seattle

Filipino immigration to the United States began after the Spanish-American War in 1898, after the Treaty of Paris, which gave the U.S. sovereignty over the Philippines.[1] For over three centuries, the Philippines had been a Spanish colony heavily influenced and controlled by the Catholic Church.[2] Then, in the latter decades of the 1800s, Dr. Jose Rizal led an organized rebellion against colonial rule, demanding greater representation and civil rights, and less taxation. Dr. Rizal was arrested and executed in 1896 for another revolt that was actually organized by another group fighting for independence, the Katipunan. As fighting between the United States and Spain ensued in Cuba, U.S. Admiral George Dewey attacked and destroyed the Spanish fleet in Manila Bay. Shortly thereafter, Katipunan leader Emilio Aguinaldo - whom Dewey brought back from exile - declared independence for the Philippines and began setting up a government. However, when the Spanish-American War ended, Spanish troops surrendered to Americans instead of native Filipinos. Filipinos rebelled against their new colonizer in the Philippine-American War, but after several years of fighting and the capture of Aguinaldo in 1901, the conflict was quelled. Military rule of the islands was subsequently replaced with civilian rule and a policy of "benevolent assimilation."

The first Filipino immigrants were recruited to work on the sugar plantations of Hawaii. Initially they numbered in the hundreds, but their numbers grew sharply after the Gentlemen's Agreement slowed the recruitment of Japanese workers to the islands. Under the Agreement, the Japanese government agreed to restrict the immigration of Japanese laborers to Hawaii and the United States; as a result, plantation owners and others who needed cheap labor decided to recruit workers from the Philippines. By 1919, Filipino immigration to Hawaii numbered some 25,000.[3] The first recorded Filipino in Washington arrived when it was still a territory. Listed as a "Manilla," he was counted among the sawmill workers at Port Blakely's lumber mill.[4] In 1910, there were 406 Filipinos on the mainland, including 17 in the state of Washington.[5] At the beginning of that decade many came to Seattle as migratory laborers (from California, Hawaii, and directly from the Philippines) in order to work in Alaska's canneries and agricultural fields in eastern Washington, as well as farms in South Park, Renton, Kent, Auburn, and Bellevue. The unpleasant boat trip from the Philippines to Seattle took about 30 days and generally included stops in Hong Kong, Korea and Japan. Space was cramped, the ventilation poor, and the meals were lousy. Many got sick; some died.

The first Filipino settlers in Seattle were a family who arrived in 1909; the father was a black-Mexican, a former U.S. Army cavalryman married to a Filipina woman.[6] The 1920 census enumerated some 500 Filipinos in Seattle, which was about half of all the Filipinos in Washington State, and 5,603 on the U.S. mainland. Their numbers, however, increased dramatically as 3,000 arrived in the Emerald City annually to find work.

Characteristic of the Asian immigrants who came to America before them, the early Filipino immigrants were predominately male by a ratio of nearly 300 to 1. Although the ratio narrowed to 14 males to 1 female by 1930, the Filipino population in America was overwhelmingly comprised of bachelors. A good percentage of them were male students, hoping to complete their education or to find a better life in - so they were led to believe - an egalitarian society with endless opportunities. Many were Ilocanos from northern Luzon.[7] Other immigrants were children and grandchildren of Spanish-American War veterans.[8]

By 1930, the number of Filipinos jumped to some 45,200 on the mainland. According to the census, there were 3,480 Filipinos in Washington state, including 1,614 in Seattle. The Filipino population exceeded that of the Chinese in both the state and Seattle; the number of Filipinos in Seattle was actually much greater than that recorded in the census. As a migratory base, more than 3,000 came annually to Seattle to find seasonal

The Anti-Filipino Movement[1]

Seattle writer Carlos Bulosan eloquently expressed the disappointment of Filipinos upon meeting prejudice in America: "Western people are brought up to regard Oriental or colored peoples as inferior, but the mockery of it all is that Filipinos are taught to regard Americans as our equals...the terrible truth is America shatters the Filipinos' dream of fraternity."

Al Magisat, who came to Seattle from Ilocos Norte Province in 1927, recalls the inequity: "When you go to the theater, you pay the same price, but you can't sit any place that you want. There is a place for Orientals only, for colored people only... And most of all they don't like us to speak to the white people, white girls. If we speak to white girl, there was always a fight." [2]

Between 1918 and 1930, anti-Filipino violence rose dramatically throughout the West Coast, much of it occurring in Washington State. The economic pressures of the Great Depression increased animosity toward Filipinos. Harassment and beatings became more commonplace.

On November 8, 1927, an irate mob of 300 whites in the Yakima Valley demanded that Filipinos leave the Valley by November 10. Kay and Polly Ibatuan and other Filipino residents were terrorized and beaten. Houses were vandalized. Filipino families gathered apprehensively at the homes of white friends until the mob was broken up by police at the urging of the federal government.

In January 1929, a labor organizer for the American Federation of Labor warned the Seattle Central Labor Council of an onslaught of Filipinos and called for their exclusion.[3] "The situation is bad in California and it is becoming increasingly bad here," he said. " In the San Joaquin Valley there are said to be 7,000 Filipinos. We

are getting the same in this state. The Yakima Valley is being overrun with them. The gates of the Pacific Coast are open to them as the law now stands. But they should be excluded." At the same labor council meeting, a letter was read by a former union member of the Filipino threat. "Second Avenue [in Seattle] is beginning to look like a street in Manila," he wrote.

"In Grays Harbor, the Filipinos are supplanting white workmen in the sawmills.

There have been problems in Toppenish. The Filipinos are everywhere in the food industry and are crowded into the steamship lines. Moreover, the Filipinos are a narcotics menace and generally are not an elevating influence on our young people. Many are marrying white girls. Those dance halls below Yesler Way, which were formerly places of entertainment for loggers and seafaring men, now are infested with South Sea Sheiks. Labor cannot stand by idly and watch these intruders take their place in our industries."

Filipinos were classified as American "nationals." As "nationals," they owed their allegiance to the United States; they were entitled to American protection. They traveled with U.S. passports and escaped the exclusionary legislation aimed at stopping the entry of other Asian immigrants to the States. Yet even their elevated legal status did not protect them fully. The burden of loyalty to America did not also carry a full range of corresponding benefits. As non-citizens, Filipinos living in the U. S. were not permitted to vote in American elections. In some jurisdictions – including Washington State – they were not permitted to own land, while in others, they were strictly forbidden to marry interracially.

The thousands of Filipino immigrants in the 1920s and 1930s found their existence circumscribed by a web of political and legal hostility. Tolerated as itinerant labor in West

Coast agriculture and Alaskan canneries, they found few opportunities elsewhere. In the cities where they rested from their seasonal work, the boundaries of Filipino enclaves were specifically marked. Whether it was King Street in Seattle or Temple Street in Los Angeles, the urban world of Filipinos was dismally consistent: hundreds of tiny rooms in rows of cheap hotels. For most of the inhabitants, the rooms were little more than places to sleep.

Yet the first generation Filipinos wanted more than the little they were offered. Products of an American educational system imposed on the Philippines, they responded with unbounded enthusiasm. Carlos Bulosan, in his classic work, *America Is In The Heart*, recalled his youthful fascination with the story of Abraham Lincoln:

"A poor boy becomes a president of the United States. Deep down in me something was touched, was springing out, demanding to be born, to be given a name. I was fascinated by the story of this boy who was born in a log cabin and became a president of the United States."[4]

Bulosan's fascination was understandable. The attractive simplicity of the Lincoln fable contrasted sharply with the poverty of Filipino rural life. America meant hope, and in the 1920s and 1930s, thousands of young Filipino men followed that hope to its source.

Unfortunately for Bulosan and his fellow voyagers, the fascination was not mutual. The America of that day was tightly governed by rules of race. On the West Coast in particular, the hostility against Asian newcomers was intense. West Coast agitation had led to the passage of federal legislation which severely restricted the immigration of first the Chinese (1882), then the Japanese (1924). It was a pervasive marker of hostility that Filipinos, despite the theoretical protection of "national" status, could not evade.

In Congress in the early 1930s, anti-Filipino sentiment was reflected in the mood to grant the Philippines independence. Although there were other forces responsible for independence, there is little doubt that American racism played a major role. As federal wards, Filipinos could not be legally prevented from coming to American shores. The answer for some was Philippine independence. This development would create a change in status from national to alien, which would then enable Congress to exclude Filipinos constitutionally. This is what transpired in 1934, with passage of the Tydings-McDuffie Act (the Philippine Independence Act). The Act provided for a 10-year period of transition to independence. During that time, a quota of 50 immigrants a year was imposed. At the end of transition, the Philippines would become independent, and Filipinos would become aliens subject to the exclusionary whim of Congress.

Yet, despite the fluctuations in the status and the overall hostility to their presence, most of the early immigrants were determined to stay in America. For many this determination meant that confinement in the cheap hotels of Chinatown, though acceptable for the present, would no longer suffice.

In Washington State, the problem was that Chinatown's segregation was reinforced by law. The 1921 Anti-Alien Land Law was designed to prevent aliens "ineligible to citizenship by naturalization" from owning land. Within the context of those times, only whites and blacks could be naturalized. All others (Japanese, Filipinos, Chinese) were specifically excluded. This law underscored a dominant American theme: Asians were tolerated only insofar as they constituted a transient, cheap labor force. In Seattle, the single room hotels of Chinatown visibly embodied that attitude.

In 1939 Pio DeCano, a Filipino immigrant in Seattle, purchased a tract of land. This act was one of the first steps taken towards establishing a permanent Filipino presence; the purchase itself reflected the deep Filipino desire for a continuing presence in the city. The purpose of the tract was its future use as a site for a Filipino Community clubhouse. Immediately, the State Attorney General's Office contested the purchase, contending that DeCano had violated the Anti-Alien Land Act.

DeCano won at both the trial court and on appeal. In neither case did the courts restrict the right of the state to limit land ownership racially. Directly successful challenges to racial restrictions had to await the post-war years of dramatic political and social change. Rather, the basis of the triumph was technical in nature: as a Filipino, Mr. DeCano did not fit the "alien" category. As a national, his allegiance was to the United States. Thus, the provisions of the law, in regard to Mr. DeCano and the Filipinos of Washington State, were inapplicable.

1. Much of the article adapted from Chin and Bacho, The International District, International Examiner, 1984.

2. Takami, *Shared Dreams*.

3. *Seattle Star* article reprinted in *Filipino Forum*, January 15, 1929.

4. Carlos Bulosan, *America is in the Heart*, University of Washington Press. Seattle 1981. page 69.

Filipino laborers.
Cannery workers'
union photo.

work in fruit orchards, berry and hop farms, mines, lumber mills, and Alaskan canneries.[9] Many returned to Seattle when their summer work was completed, and stayed over the winter months.

Filipinos were an attractive labor force because of their unique legal status. They were classified as "Nationals" and traveled with U.S. passports, unlike the Chinese and Japanese, whose immigration to the States was restricted because of exclusionary laws or bilateral agreements between nations. Filipinos could enter the United States freely until 1934, when the Philippines was given its independence under the Tydings-McDuffie Act (the Philippine Independence Act). No longer under the control of the United States, Filipinos were treated like other Asian nationals under the U.S. immigration law of 1924, and restricted to a quota of 50 immigrants per year.

Destination King Street

For the new Filipino immigrants and migrants, their destination in Seattle was the International District, where they could find some solace, familiar faces, and diversion from the laborious journey ahead. The Eastern Hotel on Maynard Avenue, the Alps Hotel and LMV (Luzon, Mindanao, and Visayas) Hotel on King Street, and the New Manila Hotel were primary stopping places for Filipino migrants, who filled the single-room unit hotels during spring and winter, upon their return from migrant seasonal labor.

The LMV Hotel and New Manila Hotel were leased and operated by the LMV Trading Company, Inc., which was probably the largest Filipino enterprise in the city in the 1920s and early 1930s. It also operated an employment agency, functioning as a labor and cannery contractor. Its advertisement in The Filipino Forum newspaper in 1929 claimed: "Labor Contractors, Pioneer Filipino Corporation. For a decade we have supplied only efficient labor." Other prominent labor and cannery contractors were the Philippine Investment Company, Salmon Cannery Contractors, Inc. and the Soon-

Dioniso Company. Pedro Santos headed the Philippine Investment Company, which was located at Eighth Avenue and King Street. The Salmon Cannery Contractors, also located on King Street, ran a billboard and pool hall onsite and also provided transportation, post office, dry cleaning, and laundry services.

King Street and its adjacent streets were clearly the core area for Filipino commerce in the city in the 1920s and 30s. Rizal Hall (near Sixth and King Street) was like a Filipino community center where lively music played constantly. The Manila Corporation Restaurant at Sixth Avenue and King Street served Filipino and Spanish dishes, and operated a pool hall next door. The business was also a cannery and labor contractor, which really blossomed after Pio DeCano became its manager in the latter 1920s. The Philippine Cafe, started and owned by Bibiana Montante Laigo, was another popular restaurant in the district during the 1930s, as was the New Manila Cafe at Maynard Avenue and King Street (the current site of Hing Hay Park). The V.M. Laigo

Company (at Sixth Avenue and King Street) was the only Filipino grocery in the city in the 1920s and 30s. The owner, Valeriano Laigo, was also a labor contractor.

It was common to see Filipino laborers gathered in hotel lobbies, barber shops, and on the street corners of the District to exchange gossip, read newspapers, and catch up on the latest news. King Street in the 1930s was like a barrio in the Philippines, noted visiting Filipino journalist Willy Torin:

Before 8 AM Chinatown is dead. At 10 AM the crowd begins to form around street corners and in the lobby of the Alps Hotel. By noon King Street is like a barrios street in the Philippines...Filipino pool halls open, [offering] diversion of pool and cards...Labor's latest news is read and discussed...Seven o'clock in the evening and...the barber shops begin to get busy...Jackson street is like Second avenue during a parade. The boys from uptown come to get down to business - lotteries, the card games, the sicoy-sicoy, et al... [By 10 PM the] tantalizing music at Rizal Hall...the crowd moves around...There is pleasure in them thar houses...[By 1 AM Rizal Hall closes, but] the Atlas Theatre is open all night.[10]

Victims of racial discrimination and exploitation, Filipinos found refuge in the International District, if only for a short moment.

Filipinos and Labor Organizing

It was also in the District's hotels that labor organizing fermented and where Carlos Bulosan (who later became a noted writer) and other Filipino labor leaders sharpened their tactics to achieve equal working conditions and fair wages for farm and cannery workers.

Filipinos began working in the canneries in 1911.[11] Gradually they replaced Chinese and Japanese cannery workers and within a decade there were more Filipinos working in the canneries of Alaska than any other ethnic group except whites and Native Alaskans. In 1928, there were nearly 4,000 Filipinos working in Alaska's canner-

---

Filipino Organizations and Lodges

The Filipino Community of Seattle (FCS), Inc., was officially established in 1935, although it actually existed as early as 1926.[1] It was an umbrella organization that included fraternities, clubs and associations. The Filipino Commerce and Labor Council and the Filipino Federation of America, Inc., which were active in the 1920s, were forerunners to the FCS.

The Filipinos established social organizations, fraternities based on provincial origin, dialect and profession.[2] The Caballeros de Dimas Alang, started in San Francisco in 1920 and one of the first Filipino lodges in Seattle, was one of several large fraternal lodges housed in the International District. It was conveniently located at the Manila Hotel. In 1928, Dimas-Alang headed the Rizal Day Movement, a national convention held at Broadway High School. The convention concluded with a well-attended Rizal Day Celebration that included speeches by the mayor and other elected officials.

Among the other larger lodges in the area were Legimaries del Trabajo and Gran Oriente Filipino.[3]

In the 1920s, a Filipino Catholic club was established under the guidance and supervision of Mr. L. J. Easterman, a Seattle attorney. The club acquired a house in the Central Area which provided room and board for workers and students attending local colleges and high schools.

While most of the Filipino immigrants who came directly by boat ended up in the International District, some students were fortunate enough to stay at a club house for Filipino students at the University of Washington. Established in 1925, the club was a few blocks from the university campus. Initially established in connection with the Filipino Catholic Club, it then attempted to run on its own. In addition to providing room and board for students, it helped them find jobs.4 Trinidad Rojo, who later became a leader in Seattle's Filipino community, was one such immigrant who came to America as a student and stayed at the house.

In the grandest bash of the decade, a thousand Filipinos celebrated the coronation of the 1927 Rizal Day Queen, Nancy Encarnacion, with a fancy downtown ball.

1. Fred Cordova. Filipino Americans: Forgotten Asian Americans. DPPA. Seattle, WA. 1983. pg. 177
2. David Takami, *Shared Dreams: A History of Asian and Pacific American in Washington State*, 1990.
3. Cordova. pg. 180.
4. Nancy Ordona Koslosky, *Filipinos in Washington. International Examiner*. June 1976.

Victorio Velasco and the Early Filipino Press

One of the leaders in Seattle's Filipino community from its beginnings was Victorio A. Velasco. As a child, he loved to write stories and poetry and was 21 years old when he quit his job as a reporter with the *Manila Times* to further his education in America. He arrived in Seattle in 1924 and soon became founder and editor of *The Philippine Seattle Colonist*, the first Filipino newspaper in the area. The paper ran until 1927. Velasco was also a member of the Filipino Students Club, attending local schools, and worked in the canneries in the summer. He eventually earned a Bachelors' and Masters' of Arts from the University of Washington.

In 1928, Velasco founded and became editor of *The Filipino Forum*, a bi-monthly publication. It called itself the "Community Newspaper of Filipinos in Seattle,"

and covered news from the Philippines as well as news about the local Filipino community. The paper's office was at Fifth Avenue and South Main Street. This paper ran until 1937, when it suspended publication, but resumed printing after World War II.

Velasco, who lived in the International District, was active in community organizations throughout his life, including the Jackson Street Community Council. Velasco is credited with changing the name of the Seattle Filipino Clubhouse Fund (a fund to build a center for Filipino students at the University of Washington) to Filipino Community of Seattle, Inc., in order to build a center for the entire Filipino community. The center was acquired in 1965 on what is now Martin Luther King Way. A cannery worker and union member who once held office, Velasco was tragically burned to death in 1968 when he tried to retrieve his typewriter from the bunkhouse at a cannery in Alaska.

In 1933, *The Filipino American Tribune* was established by the Cannery Workers and Field Laborers Union (CWFLU), American Federation of Labor Local 18257, which later became Local 37 Cannery Workers Union. The *Tribune*'s editor was Emiliano Francisco; the paper provided local news as well as news about the canneries and union. Over the paper's 60-year history it became an enterprise owned by Francisco. Its name also changed; it was initially called the *The Filipino American Tribune*, then the *Filipino Tribune*, the *Filipino Courier* and finally the *Filipino-American Herald*.

A rival newspaper called the *Philippine Advocate* was published from 1934 to 1937 by the Filipino Protective Laborers Association. Other local Filipino newspapers that appeared before 1950 were the *Seattle Filipino Outlook*, *Northwest Forum*, and *Philippine Review*.

---

ies compared to 1,065 Chinese, 1,445 Japanese, and 1,269 Mexicans.[12] At its peak in the 1950s and 1960s, six to seven thousand Filipinos made the trek to Alaska.

Initially, Filipinos were recruited to the canneries by Chinese and Japanese labor contractors, but Filipino labor contractors emerged by 1914.[13] Pedro Santos was the first Filipino labor contractor, delivering some 500 workers annually for the New England Fish Company. Perhaps the best-known Filipino labor contractor was Pio DeCano, Sr.[14] Taking over the cannery operations of Valeriano Sarasal in 1926, DeCano directly employed 70 workers. He also supplied another 600 cannery workers

to canneries in Sand Point, Drier Bay, Kake, Port San Juan, and Uganik in southeast Alaska.

Labor contractors for the canneries were responsible for recruiting, hiring, feeding and supervising the workers. Contractors also hired cooks, purchased food for the mess halls, kept track of the workers' time, and paid them at the end of the season. The canneries provided transportation to the work site and housing in Alaska. Labor contracting was competitive, since contractors bid against one another to provide work crews. It was a repressive system that fostered worker exploitation and conflict. Nonetheless, the

Filipino immigrants - like the Chinese and Japanese before them - had little choice since American society relegated them to being migrant seasonal or service workers.

Filipinos who spent the summers in the canneries of Alaska were called "Alaskeros." Cannery work - cleaning, processing and canning salmon - was difficult and shunned by most. Hours generally ran from 6 in the morning until 6 at night, six days a week; it was not uncommon to begin work earlier or to end work at 10 or 11 p.m.. The Filipino workers were typically housed in separate, run-down barracks, and ate poor food at different mess halls with different menus than whites. Safety and sanitary conditions were extremely poor, as was the pay. Cannery work paid $70 per month for old-timers and $60 for newer workers in the late 1920s. Furthermore, the cannery workers took these jobs without a chance of getting promoted to higher paying non-cannery positions. Winter and spring meant working in the asparagus and lettuce fields, and later the fruit and grape fields in California. In Washington, Filipinos were employed on farms around Kent, Auburn, Woodinville, South Park, Renton, and Bellevue and on farms further east in Yakima, Wapato, and Toppenish.[15]

In 1930-1931, Filipinos had been attacked for driving down wages; soon they would be found trying to raise them. Workers threatened a strike in March 1935, which was averted when the Japanese Growers' Association agreed to a 47 percent increase in pay. Shunned and taunted by organized labor, local Filipinos had taken it upon themselves to form the Filipino Labor Association five years earlier. Joe de Guzman was elected president of the organization and Vincent Aget (a labor contractor), its vice-president.

Creating a labor association was a big step. Creating a labor union was an even bigger step and much more difficult. The new immigrants had to overcome not only the animosity of organized labor towards non-whites, but also had to learn the basic functions, structure and membership responsibilities of a labor union. Labor unions did not exist in the Philippines and were consequently an unfamiliar concept to the new immigrants. Furthermore, it was a challenge to get a seasonal migrant workforce dispersed throughout California, Eastern Washington, and Alaska to participate in a permanent year-round union.[16]

Nevertheless, in 1933, Virgil Duyungan, a 1926 graduate of Broadway High School, applied to the State Federation of Labor for a charter to form a union. The charter was granted. The Cannery Workers and Farm Laborers Union, Local 18257, which later became Local 37 of the American Federation of Labor, was chartered on June 19th. Duyungan was the union's first president, and the union hall had a storefront at Fifth Avenue and South Washington Street. A short time later, Congress passed the 1933 National Recovery Act. The hearings, held in San Francisco that summer, investigated labor practices in the salmon canning industry. Labor practices in the salmon canning industry were investigated during the hearings, which were held in San Francisco that summer. The passage of the National Recovery Act led to the demise of the labor contracting system in the canneries.

By 1936, the new union had 3,000 members of different ethnic groups, mostly Filipinos and Japanese. Before then, however, an opposition faction within the union, suspicious of Duyungan's insistence that membership dues be paid before sailing to Alaska, started the Filipino Protective Laborers Association. After a series of mediation meetings, Duyungan and the union were charged with accepting money from cannery operators to keep their workers' memberships current. An election was subsequently held in which Duyungan defeated the opposition to remain in office. However, Duyungan was assassinated in 1936 along with two other officers of the union. Duyungan shot the assassin, Baseda Patron - the nephew of a labor contractor - in self-defense.

In 1937, some Filipino workers, frustrated with the AFL because of its racial discrimination and lack of support, affiliated themselves with the Congress of Industrial Organizations (CIO) United Cannery, Agricultural, Packinghouse and Allied Workers of America Local 7. Trinidad Rojo became its president in 1939, when the union was on the verge of bankruptcy. Under then-president I.R. Cabatit, previous union officers had charged personal items to union accounts. Rojo took charge and immediately eliminated half of the staff positions, drastically reduced the officers' wages, and held several fundraisers to keep the organization afloat. Despite his success, Rojo turned

In Memoriam

VIRGIL S. DUYUNGAN, First President

Killed by enemies of Organized Labor on December 1, 1936, our late brothers, Virgil S. Duyungan and Aurelio A. Simon, made the Supreme Sacrifice

"That Union Hiring Might Be Established in the Canned Salmon Industry."

RICARDO GABO   NICK BALTAZAR
DEMAS GABRIEL   PETE SANTOS
AURELIO A. SIMON   MILTON HEDRICK

down the opportunity to become union president the following year and handed the office to Vincente O. Navea. A decade later, the union became the Food, Tobacco and Allied Workers of America (FTA) Local 7 of the CIO and, in 1950, it was renumbered Local 37.

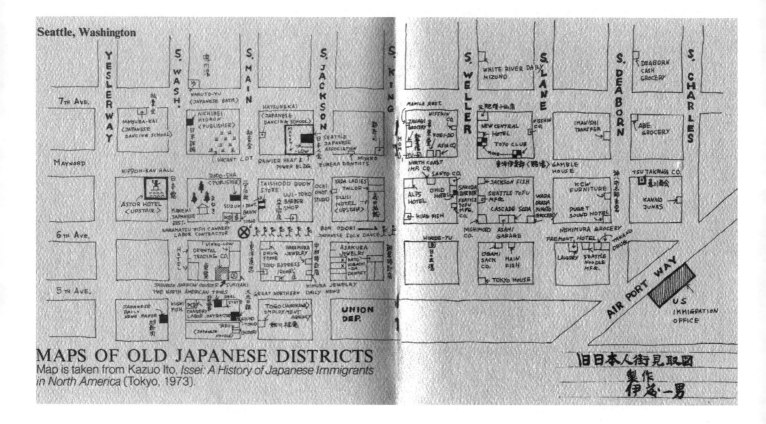

MAPS OF OLD JAPANESE DISTRICTS

Map is taken from Kazuo Ito, *Issei: A History of Japanese Immigrants in North America* (Tokyo, 1973).

Part Six: The Heyday of the 20s through the depression

The Roaring 20s

As the Filipino presence in the area emerged, so did the presence of African Americans. At the same time, the Japanese and Chinese sectors continued their growth as well, creating a lively and robust district. In many ways, it was a multiracial area in its heyday, experiencing the good times of the "Roaring 20s."

E. Russell "Noodles" Smith and Burr "Blackie" Williams, two African Americans, opened the Dumas Club, a social club for blacks, in 1917 at Tenth Avenue and Jackson Street.[1] Three years later, Smith and Jimmy Woodland opened the Entertainers Club at Twelfth and Jackson Street, where they started the Alhambra nightclub in the basement in 1922; the Alhambra became the Black and Tan in 1932. "Noodles" Smith was a gambler and businessman who came to Seattle during the Alaska Yukon Pacific Exposition in 1909. He also opened the Golden West and Coast Hotel in the International District, where such celebrities as Louis Armstrong, Duke Ellington, and Erskine Hawkins stayed. Other African American nightclubs, hotels and businesses opened in the District over the decades.

Chinese Americans also continued to be active in the area. In 1921, news of a famine in China spread throughout the community. A large campaign and festival were held in Chinatown to raise money and collect supplies and goods to send back to China. In 1922, a new Chinese Baptist Church was erected in Chinatown, on Tenth Avenue and King Street (missionaries had founded the church at Fifth Avenue and Yesler Way in 1896, later moving it to Washington Street). The church was a magnet for social as well as religious activities in the community, especially for the second generation. One of the key programs the Baptist Church ran was a nursery school. Virtually every Chinese child in the city, Christian or not, attended the nursery and could remember their first taste of graham crackers and milk there.

The first Chinese newspaper in Seattle, the Chinese Star, was established in 1925. Four people worked on the weekly publication, including Willard Jue, who had recently arrived from Portland and was a student at the University of Washington. The newspaper, which covered news from China and the local community, was supported by the Nationalist Chinese government and ran for four years. Thereafter, the local non-English-reading Chinese depended on Chinese newspapers from Vancouver and San Francisco for information about China and the outside world.

THE ROOTS OF JAZZ IN SEATTLE
by Paul de Barros
with photographs by Eduardo Calderón

JACKSON STREET
AFTER HOURS

By 1925, only a handful of Chinese businesses, including a few gambling joints, remained in the old Chinatown area around Second and Washington Street. Most of the Chinese gambling and lottery houses, by then, were prevalent in the new Chinatown, with some stores selling cigarettes as a front. Chinese and others would go to gamble in the back rooms, and lottery tickets were sold to all who were willing to take the gamble. To non-Chinese, Seattle's Chinatown was a place to eat Chinese food, gamble, play the lottery and enjoy the nightlife. It had a reputation as a place for wild entertainment, especially

Memories of Nisei sports clubs (excerpted)

(Mayumi Tsutakawa, *International Examiner*, July 1976)

For Japanese immigrants and their children, sports such as baseball served as both recreational and social institutions. Over the years, thousands of young Nisei men and women played baseball, basketball and football in teams and leagues organized in the Japanese community throughout the state....Shig Osawa, one of the oldest Nisei in Seattle, tells of sandlot baseball games at 5th and Main dating the turn of the century. The few Japanese and Chinese kids in the neighborhood at that time played catch all the way to South School, the old Bailey Gatzert, and home. Occasionally, Osawa recalls, they challenged "a team of white kids from up on 10th and Main."

There was often no money even for a ball, so Osawa "got up 5 cents and bought a rubber ball." Then he wrapped twine around it many times, and sewed a cloth cover with a darning needle. When they couldn't find a nickel, they even tried using a rock, wrapping the twine over it.

In 1906, the first Japanese baseball team was established: the Nippon Club, composed of young Issei men who toiled in typical immigrant jobs in canneries, janitorial, and domestic service. At about the same time, the Columbia Club from Tacoma, the Hayato, a Kagoshima group and the Mikado team started up.

Trips to Japan were made during this early time and games with Japanese college teams were held. The Nippon, Mikado and Columbia clubs went to Japan in 1914.

Perhaps the first Nisei team to organize was the Cherries, started by Mr. Doi in 1911. Doi got Osawa to play. The next year some Mikado people left that team and joined some Cherry team members to form the Asahi Club.

The Asahis became the strongest team and rivalry with the Mikados was intense.

International Examiner file photo.

According to Osawa, legitimate businesses favored the Asahis, but the Shitamachi (underworld), represented by the Toyo gambling club, favored the Mikado. Heavy game betting led to controversy over an umpire's decision at a championship game. A fight ensued and a gun was pulled, said Kenji Kawaguchi, former sports player. Osawa said the betting involved high stakes such as automobiles.

By 1919, the Asahi and Mikados each had three teams even though the Asahi were having financial trouble....[Tura Nakamura, George Ishihara, and Osawa]

put the team into a newly formed semi-pro league and traveled to play teams in other towns, as far away as Montana and Spokane. Through conservative management of funds, the team earned enough to travel and to make up for back debts.

By 1924, Mr. Miyasawa was able to unite the two clubs, the Mikados and Asahis, into the new Nippon Athletic Club, taking the best players from both teams. By this time, football and basketball were added to the activities. In 1926, the Taiyo Club was started, accommodating the next best players in the community.

Kenjiro Yoshino, one of the few young Issei on the Taiyo team, said most parents favored the second generation's preoccupation with such a good, clean sport as baseball. "It kept the kids out of mischief," he said. Most Issei parents, though they had not played baseball in Japan, enthusiastically attended league games and championships and cheered their sons to victory.

The *Japanese American Courier*, a Nisei newspaper published by James Sakamoto, sponsored an athletic league from 1928 until the war broke out. It included baseball, basketball and football sections. It also included a girls' basketball league. Coaches volunteered their time.

The Fourth of July brought the annual Japanese state baseball championship at Columbia Field, now the Rainier Playfield. An all-weekend event, it brought hundreds of Nikkei out to enjoy the vendors, booths and games. Started in the late 30s, it continued until the war broke out.

Toward the end of the 30s and early 40s, sports interests were changing, and some older Nisei started taking up golf and fishing, according to some old Taiyo members. Only one Taiyo team entered league competition in 1941.

After the war, the teams were not started up again because "everyone was too busy," according to Kawaguchi. Yoshino pointed out that many community leaders who had helped out with the youth teams were now more concerned with survival matters such as gaining back property, businesses and finding homes for their families after the war.

Yoshino said the start of Little League after the war took many Japanese youngsters away from the possible start of a new team. Of course, many Sansei today are concerned more with basketball, Yoshino conceded.

Tad Kuniyuki, another former Taiyo player, feels much respect is due the Sakamotos—James and his wife Misao—for the many hours they put into their newspaper, making the Courier Leagues possible. A former sports writer for the *Courier*, Kuniyuki said the Sakamotos spent countless unrewarded hours for the sake of the young second generation....

among Fort Lewis soldiers and Navy personnel with shore passes. Bottle clubs, dance halls and prostitution houses added to the glamour of the area in the 1920s and 30s.

Some Chinese businesses, such as import/export businesses that supplied Chinese restaurants, were able to survive solely on a Chinese clientele. However, most Chinese businesses - including restaurants, hand laundries and curio shops - relied on a large base of non-Chinese customers. One example was Charlie Louie's Chinese Garden. Born in Portland, Louie came to Seattle in 1904, worked at a laundry and then became a bar boy at the Lincoln Hotel, eventually rising to the position of head bartender. He left the Lincoln to open the Tien Heung (Heavenly Flavor), the city's first downtown Chinese restaurant, at Third and Pike Street. His success led him to open other restaurants and a Chinese import/export establishment on King Street.

In 1923, Louie took the bold step of building a Chinese opera house on Seventh Avenue and Weller Street. He brought in talent from San Francisco and Hong Kong, but discovered that he had to resort to booking prizefights to make the place successful. Finally, in 1929, he converted the opera house into the Chinese Garden, a Chinese restaurant with a dance hall. Local drummer Leonard Gayton and his band opened the new venue in 1930.[2] It quickly became one of the city's most popular night spots, an esteemed venue where men wore ties and women wore evening gowns. Although it was shut down briefly by a federal raid a year after it opened, the Chinese Garden was regarded as one of the city's better

night spots, with consistently outstanding bands and jam sessions until its closing after World War II.

Directly across the street from the Chinese Garden was the Hong Kong Chinese Society Club, one of the more rambunctious nightclubs in the city. It was also known as the "Bucket of Blood," after a murder that occurred in front of the club after a raid.[3] Despite the rowdy crowd, the Hong Kong Chinese Society Club was a favorite of African American jazz musicians because it was a good place to jam. The Hong Kong Club and the Chinese Garden were just a few of the many outstanding jazz spots in the International District. The King Fur Cafe, Mar's Cafe and, in the 1930s and 40s, Twin Dragon Restaurant, Basin Street, Golden West Club, Tuxedo Club, Elks Club, China Pheasant and Danny Woo's New Chinatown Restaurant were also popular Chinatown night spots. Chinese-operated establishments such as the King Fur and New Chinatown often booked African American jazz musicians, as did Louie's Chinese Garden.[4]

Meanwhile, Japantown was at its peak. "The center of Nihonmachi," wrote David Takami, "was Sixth and Main. During the Bon Odori festival, a bandstand for musicians was constructed in the blocked off intersection. Main Street from Fifth to Maynard was closed for the dancing, and shop owners hung colorful Japanese lanterns outside their doors. At other times of the year, the neighborhood could have been any town in Japan. The smells of soba broth, shoyu and other Japanese foods wafted through the air. Passersby spoke Japanese. After dark, men strolled about in yukata and geta (wood slippers) to the strains of shamisen from nearby homes." On week-

James Sakamoto. International Examiner file photo.

litical participation. Nineteen persons attended that initial meeting, choosing Shigeru Osawa as the League's first president. Osawa operated an auto repair garage in what is now the International District. The Progressive Citizens League, however, did not have a strong following until former prizefighter James Sakamoto became involved.

Blinded by boxing injuries, Sakamoto started the Japanese American Courier, the first English-language newspaper in the Japanese community, in 1928. Along with his boyhood friend, Clarence Arai, Sakamoto revitalized the Progressive Citizens League, which merged with other Japanese American organizations in the country and Hawaii to form the Japanese Americans Citizens League (JACL). Sakamoto was also a leader in the formation of the national JACL, which held its first national convention in Seattle in 1930. Arai was elected the national president, the organization's first, at the convention. Sakamoto was elected the president of the Seattle Chapter in 1931 and later served as national president from 1936 to 1938.

In 1929, the Chong Wa Benevolent Association building was constructed next to the Chinese Garden on the northeast cor-

ner of Seventh Avenue and Weller Street. The Association had been housed at various locations - initially with the Chinese School on Twelfth Avenue, then in the Kong Yick Building. Later, the Association leased space on the upper floor of the Oak Tin Building (across the street on Seventh Avenue) before constructing its own building. Chong Wa was a powerful umbrella organization composed of family and district associations, and tongs. It represented the Chinese throughout the area. Many attended their monthly meetings, which were often filled to capacity. These meetings provided an important means for key figures in the community to interact, settle disputes, and establish direction for the community's welfare. The new two-story building immediately became the pride and focal point of the Chinese community. The first floor housed classrooms for the Chinese school and the upper floor had a large auditorium with a stage. Chinese American dignitaries from all over the United States attended the opening of the building. Dong Shi Chun (also known as Dong On Long) was the president at the time. Until World War II, the Chinese enjoyed a high degree of "extra-territoriality" from the rest of Seattle. Chong Wa, an umbrella association consisting of a large number of local Chinese organizations, acted as the main governing body. Chinatown was left alone to govern its own affairs.

The Depression Era

Frank Miyamoto, describing the Japanese community in the 1930s, wrote:

Here near Fifth and Sixth Avenues on Main and Jackson Streets, is the business center of the Japanese district, consisting of a

ends, Japanese from areas outside of the city flocked to Nihonmachi, appreciably increasing the commerce and activity there. In 1930, 12 import/export dealers led the local Japanese economy with earnings at some $7.7 million, followed by 100 groceries with $3.5 million, and hotel at $1.6 million. Some 905 Japanese businesses that year brought in a total of $24 million.[5]

The Seattle Progressive Citizens League was started on September 27, 1921, to carry out recreational, social and educational programs. It later focused on community unity, heritage, citizenship, assimilation, and po-

Goon Dip

Adding to the hardship of the Depression was the loss of one of the Chinese community's greatest leaders. In 1933 Goon Dip, the "Merchant Prince," known for his generosity, died.

Goon Dip had arrived in Portland in 1876 at the age of 14. He subsequently worked as a general laborer on the railroads in Tacoma and Montana. He returned to Toisan to marry, but upon his return found himself without a job. However, a sympathetic American woman took him home and convinced her parents to hire Goon as a houseboy. She later taught him English.

Goon then found employment with Moy Bok-Hin, a millionaire businessman and labor contractor. Goon's bilingual ability provided a valuable communication tool in business dealings and transactions, paving the way to higher responsibilities within Moy's company.

By 1900, having gained experience in business, Goon Dip left Moy's business and started his own general dry goods store with a hemstitching operation that hired disabled Chinese. By using important business connections, established while working for Moy, Goon Dip also contracted labor, supplying cooks and cannery workers for the Oregon-Washington Railroad and Navigation Company (which operated riverboats and canneries).

Goon Dip was appointed Honorary Chinese Consul for the Northwest in 1908, re-

Goon Dip, the "Merchant Prince." Wing Luke Asian Museum photo.

placing his former employer Moy Bok-Hin. He moved to Seattle from Portland in 1909, while organizing and working on the China Exhibit at Alaska-Yukon-Pacific Exhibition in Seattle. At the Exhibition, Goon met E.B. Deming, who had just purchased Pacific American Fisheries (a large salmon cannery in south Bellingham). Goon became the sole labor contractor for Deming. Eventually, Pacific American Fisheries became the world's largest salmon cannery, with more than a dozen canneries in Washington and Alaska. Goon Dip was to become rich.

In 1911, he constructed the Milwaukee Hotel at South King Street and Seventh Avenue. His family and his office occupied the top floor of the building, which was the largest hotel in the area at the time.

Around 1918, Goon Dip joined Bernard Hirst and S.W. Fries to form the Hirst Chichagof Mine near Juneau, Alaska. Many local Chinese purchased shares in the venture, which turned a profit until the Depression. Taxes and other revenues produced by the mining operation helped keep the Alaska territorial government afloat. As a tribute, a mountain and a river on Chichagof Island were named after Goon Dip.

In the community, Goon Dip actively participated in the Kong Yick Investment Company and Chong Wa Benevolent Association and its Chinese school.

When he passed away, the city witnessed one of its biggest funerals, and Chinatown mourned for days.

Prostitution and Gambling

At the turn of the century the International District inhabitants, including the Japanese, were mostly single men. Socially deviant enterprises emerged to exploit this situation —most noticeably, prostitution and gambling.

The presence of Japanese prostitutes did not persist without evoking a strong reaction from the community. Around 1904 a movement, spearheaded by Japanese churches, succeeded in driving a "Japanese colony" of prostitutes into rural areas. The presence of such women on payday at outlying sawmills was not uncommon.

Japanese women were shipped to the Seattle area to work in its brothels and outlying areas where there were work gangs. The brothels were initially situated around Second and Occidental Avenues; after 1910, they were located from Jackson Street to King Street on Maynard Avenue, and along Weller Street between Fifth and Seventh Avenues.

It was reported that there were 200 Japanese prostitutes alone. About half of them catered to Japanese only, while the others made no distinction.

Perhaps the most noted prostitute was Waka Yamada, a noted writer in Japan, who was lured to America by tales of great wealth.[1] She operated under the name of "Oyae of Arabia."

Gambling, which was legal at the time, regularly occurred wherever there were large gangs of workers, both in the city and rural areas. Organized groups of gambling operators appeared at work camps, usually on payday, to test the workers' luck and prey on the workers' dreams.

The Chinese started their own gambling clubs, followed by the Japanese. The first Japanese club, the Jinai Club, was started in 1917. The largest in the area was the Toyo Club, which began in the early 1920s. The Toyo Club was initially located at the northeast corner of Maynard Avenue and Lane Street and later moved to the New Central Building (immediately to the north), where it occupied the entire second floor. It was purported to be the second largest gambling establishment on the West Coast at the time. Gambling occurred throughout the International District, but was concentrated mostly on King and Weller Streets.

Competition for customers was keen and somewhat based on ethnicity. It was not uncommon, for instance, to find gambling operators castigating members of their own ethnic group for patronizing a gambling hall owned by members of another ethnic group. In the 1930s, for instance, Filipino leaders complained bitterly of Chinese gambling establishments. "Issuance of millions of lottery tickets every week," read the headlines of one of the Filipino newspapers in the city. "Secret passage are available in these joints leading a victim to safe exit to escape the law." Filipinos in an aggregate of one million dollars payroll lost 50% of their earnings in these places every year. Secretary Mislang of the Cannery Workers and Farm Workers Union remarked: "These gambling establishments are the ones responsible for driving hundreds

bunch of shops including everything from barber shops and restaurants to book stores and law offices. The business center is not today what it was in the heyday of the early nineteen-twenties, when Main Street really teemed with the life of the incoming immigrants and prosperous farmers visiting town. Rather is one aware now that the depression has not dealt kindly with the shopkeepers; that the failure of one community's bank, and the large movements of their population back to Japan, and even more to California, have drained the lifeblood out of the community.[6]

According to a 1935 report by the Japanese Chamber of Commerce, there were 2,867 Japanese in the Japantown area.[7] Most worked in the trades or provided services at hotels, groceries, dye works, public market stands, produce houses, gardening, restaurants, barber shops, and laundries. The Depression, in the early 1930s, was especially hard on the community. The Japanese population in Seattle dropped from 8,448 in 1930 to some 6,975 in 1940. Many

moved to other areas or returned to Japan. The restriction on immigration also helped blunt the growth of the Japanese community.

In 1931, news of Japan's invasion of Manchuria aroused the Chinese community in Seattle. At a community meeting, Chinese decided to boycott Japanese stores in the area to express their anger. Not all Chinese complied, however, and those who didn't were reprimanded before the community.

of Filipinos into the breadline every winter, and if the authorities will permit, our organization will place pickets on these places around August 15 to save our members from losing their money to Mr. Chinaman."

Ray Chinn, who grew up in the District and whose family operated the Wa Sang Company for decades on King Street, described the lottery scene in the 1930s: "The main lottery was in Chinatown. I always remember they used to have drawings at 12 o'clock, 2 o'clock, 4 o'clock and then 9 o'clock or something—about four drawings a day. And, of course whenever it's close to drawing time, they have all these runners coming to the area. I remember different stores would have these lottery tickets underneath somewhere. There were afraid the police might arrest them. All these big stores would have a cigar store in the front. They never sell any cigars. It's all in the back. But people go in there to buy lottery tickets. Sometimes, they get a raid. Usually they have somebody in headquarters who would forewarn them. All of a sudden, I will see guys pouring out of the back doors of these places".[2]

Gambling, liquor and prostitution were illegal but clearly a huge part of the District's economy in the 20s, 30s and 40s. Vice in the District and in the city was allowed in exchange for regular pay to policemen and other officials. "In Seattle, there was no 'mob,'" wrote Paul de Barros in explaining the illegal activity that occurred in the Seattle nightclubs. "The boys in blue were on the take. The amusing colloquial name for this institutional graft was the 'tolerance policy,' which meant that in exchange for police 'tolerance' of alcohol, gambling, and prostitution, operators would pay fixed prices on a regular basis."[3] Phony raids were even carried out to make it appear that law enforcement was clamping down on illegal activity at nightclubs. Police would call in advance and an employee would be designated as the person to be arrested. The arrested person, usually the bartender (who had already been fingerprinted), would go to the jailhouse and sign in, and be back at the nightclub in an hour.

In 1949, an initiative was passed that allowed hard liquor by the drink. The initiative effectively led to the downfall of the "bottle clubs" (so called because one could

buy liquor at these places illegally), since it only allowed hotels and restaurants that sold food to sell liquor by the drink. The police and the state Liquor Control Board worked with the Jackson Street Community Council to close "bottle clubs" in the area.

Gambling in the District continued in various degrees until the early 1990s when the federal District Attorney General threatened to confiscate the Kong Yick Buildings for illegal gambling. While mahjongg is still played socially, high-level gambling in the District has all but ceased.

1.David Takami, *Executive Order 9066*, Wing Luke Asian Museum, 1992, p. 10.
2."Tales of the I.D.," *Seattle Times*, Feb. 27, 1994, Section L.
3. Paul de Barros, *Jackson Street After Hours*, Sasquatch Books, p.77.

During the Depression, Chinese suffered like most other Americans. Many lost their jobs; those who were fortunate enough to remain employed worked for meager wages. According to the U.S. Census data, there was no increase in the Chinese population in Seattle between 1920 and 1930. Meanwhile, the Chinese population for the state decreased to its lowest point since the beginning of Chinese immigration to Washington. There were 2,195 Chinese recorded in the state in 1930, a decrease of 168 from the previous decade and nearly 1,500 from 1900.

The decreases were, in large part, the result of exclusionary anti-Chinese immigration laws and the lack of employment opportunities. In the following decade, the Chinese population in Seattle grew to 1,781 - an increase of 434 from 1930. The increase was primarily due to natural births rather than immigration.

In 1938, the African American Elks Club moved from the Central Area to the second floor of the Rainier Power and Heat Building at Jackson and Maynard (the same building where the JACL office was located). It remained there until the early 1950s and is noted as the club where Ray Charles (then known as R.C. Robinson) got his first regular paid performance.

Restricted Mobility

As a general rule, minorities in the United States tend to occupy working class neighborhoods once they leave their initial ghettos. Asians in Seattle were no different.

Traditional Chinese organizations

The Wa Chong, Quong Tuck and Mark Ten Suie companies (and other Chinese-owned general stores) played a major role in helping meet sojourners' needs. The stores served as social gathering places and boarding houses. The sojourners slept in specially designated rooms, while the merchants' families and relatives occupied other rooms. Cooking facilities were available and meals were served at a small fee. The stores were where sojourners exchanged gossip, employment opportunities and general news and information as well as where they sent and received letters from China. Some stores also provided places to gamble.

Generally, those who used the facilities of any particular store had the same surname or common ancestry. For instance, those with the surname Chin would use the facilities of Wa Chong or Quong Tuck companies, operated by Chins; those with the surname Mar would go to a store owned by a Mar. This system reflected the social organization found in China, which was based on clans or lineage groups formed according to common ancestry and residential area. Around the turn of the century, enough Chinese immigrants from any one surname or ancestral group created more formal organizations, such as family and district associations.

The first Chinese organizations established in Seattle, however, were probably local branches of tongs headquartered in San Francisco. In a sensationalistic piece in the *Seattle Post-Intelligencer* headlined, "A Highbinder Court," the reporter told of a "hearing before the Seattle branch of the Six Companies," attended by 300 Chinese. It was held at the hall above Wa Chong's store and chaired by "Wa Chong," apparently referring to Chin Chun Hock. On trial was Ah Jim, accused by Ah How of informing the customs officers of the illegal entry of four Chinese into this country. According to the reporter, the two belonged to two rival factions, Ah Jim from a Jackson Street merchant group and Ah

Chong Wah Building

How backed by a group from Washington Street (and headed by Chin Chun Hock). Ah Jim pleaded innocent, but was found guilty and fined $15. The reporter also mentioned that the "society" was a branch with headquarters in San Francisco and warned the readers of the gangster-like character of the organization. "Ah Jim, being a member of the society and bound to obey the call or suffer death by the treacherous knife, appeared," he wrote. "Chinatown," he added, "was armed with knives, rocks and clubs."

The three basic types of associations that emerged in the larger Chinatowns of America to meet the needs of its inhabitants were: (1) family associations (clans), (2) district associations (common speech-district groups) and (3) tongs or secret societies. These associations were transplanted from China in a modified form and emerged in Seattle. Like Chong Wa, an umbrella organization comprising all of the Chinese associations in the area, all functioned benevolently: they helped their members with protection, shelter, loans, employment, settled disputes, and provided a place to congregate, burial services and a medium to carry on Chinese traditions.

In Seattle, Chinese with the same surname established local branches of family associations which were frequently centralized in San Francisco. The local associations, however, operated independently. There were also family associations which were comprised of more than one surname but had a common ancestor.

Of all the family associations in the city, the largest was the Gee How Oak Tin (Filial Piety and Brotherhood) Benevolent Association, whose members had one of several surnames: Chin (or Chan), Woo and Yuen. The large membership of this organization can be traced to the success of Chin Chun Hock and Chin Gee Hee. Their connections (with others from the same villages in Toisan and from their same clan in San Francisco) were instrumental in the settlement of the large number of Chins, Woos and Chans in Seattle. In fact, the Oak Tin Association's first meetings were held at the upper floor of the Wa Chong building at Fourth and Main, which was owned by Chin Chun Hock. The Oak Tin Association began in 1900 at that location, moved to King Street in 1913 and purchased its own building at Seventh Avenue South and Weller Street in 1921 after a national fund raising campaign led by Chin Jackman. Other family associations included the Chew, Dong, Eng, Luke, Lee Wong, and Yee.

There are four tongs that operated in Seattle: Hip Sing, Hop Sing, Suey Sing, and Bing Kung. For many years, the Bing Kung Tong was the largest and most powerful tong, wielding a great deal of influence in Chong Wa. Today, only a few older men are active in these institutions.

Over the years, membership in the family associations and tongs has drastically dwindled. In earlier years, these groups played a vital role in helping Chinese adjust and survive, especially immigrants. In recent years, however, the roles and influence of these male-dominated organizations have all but vanished.

Established sometime during the first decade of the 1900s, Chong Wa was the governing body for all the Chinese in Washington State and represented the community to the outside world. Upon news of Japan's invasion of Manchuria in 1931, Chong Wa organized a boycott of Japanese stores in the area. Those who did not participate were ostracized in the community. Through the end of World War II, Chong Wa organized numerous fundraisers to support China's war effort and to assist war victims.

During the Great Depression, Chong Wa regularly distributed food to the needy, even though the Chinese community may not have felt the impact of those times as much as other

groups. Chinese had been very adept at making do with very little, and many continued working in places where they were able to hang on to their jobs — the canneries, gambling houses and restaurants.

In the 1960s, the local Chong Wa had a board of some 49 trustee members; 27 of these were elected by a community-wide election and 22 were delegates from member organizations. The trustees then chose the officers. They formed a school board which oversaw the operations of the Chinese language school. They also started a Seafair committee which organized a Chinese Community Night during the city's Seafair festival; the events included a parade, fashion show, Chinese opera, art exhibit, bazaar, and dragon dance in Chinatown.

The annual revenues at that time were about $10,000, most of which came from direct solicitation to Chinese businesses. Another funding source was an annual fundraising dinner. The revenues raised annually were just enough to cover the costs for minimal building operations and maintenance, the school operation, the cemetery maintenance, and the Chinese girls drill team.

In the 1970s, the Chinatown Chamber of Commerce took over the role of sponsoring the Chinatown Parade at Seafair. The Chamber also promoted Chinatown by sponsoring events during Chinese New Year and the Moon Festival. The organization was started in the 1960s by Don Chin, who had a business in the area and was very active with the Jackson Street Community Council. Chin was a prime promoter of the District

since the early 1950s. The Chinatown Chamber has since changed its name to Chinese/Chinatown Chamber of Commerce, to reflect its growing membership of businesses outside of Chinatown and its interest outside of that area.

In 1938, the Luck Ngi Musical Society was founded to support war victims in China, operate the Chinese school, promote Chinese opera, and raise funds for other community causes. The club initially performed plays and later Cantonese opera. During World War II, the group put on four or five performances a year at the Chong Wa hall. In earlier days, nearly all of its members were men, many of whom lived and worked in the restaurants in the District. Men played the role of women in the operas. They honed their skills at 703 King Street, on the second floor of one of the Kong Yick buildings. There was a small stage, a cabinet with the instruments, and small rooms in the back to practice and put on makeup. Many of the members, both Chinese-born and American-born Chinese, came to the Luck Ngi club to practice after work when the restaurants closed. It was not uncommon to hear Chinese music in the wee hours of the morning.

Today, there are about 90 members in the club. Most are middle-aged and older immigrants. The singers and musicians practice together weekly, from about 9 p.m. until the early morning hours.

Jackson Street in the 1930s. Wing Luke Asian Museum photo.

Around 1920, Asians generally began to move into the Yesler Hill area, a district prominently occupied by working class whites and Jews. Other Asians began moving into the Beacon Hill area. Until World War II, however, only limited numbers of Asians moved into these areas. The bulk of those who moved were well-to-do families wanting to leave the congestion of the International District or families which could not find adequate housing there.

The "restrictive covenant" provisions restricting the sale of real estate to non-whites hampered the residential mobility of Asians. According to one Chinese, formerly employed by the Federal Housing Authority, Asians moved into the First Hill, Central Area and Beacon Hill areas because those were the only areas not covered by restrictive covenants.

The residential mobility of Asians in Seattle, particularly the Chinese, was also limited because many were men who were either sojourners, single, or married with families back in their home country. Rather than move outside the International District and pay more for housing and face the hostility of whites, they remained to enjoy what little comfort and conveniences they had. Furthermore, a number of Asian families could not afford to move out and others chose to remain within a community with an Asian cultural environment.

One of the few Chinese to graduate from college and find work in his trained profession was Helm Kee Chinn. His father, Chin We-Shing, came to America in the 1860s and worked on the railroads and then ended up at Port Blakely, where he worked at the lumber mill and operated a laundry before moving his family to Seattle. Helm Kee Chinn and his brother were among the first Chinese to graduate in engineering from the University of Washington. Helm Kee went on to receive a master's degree, the first Chinese at the university to do so. He was fortunate enough to get a job with the Army Corps of Engineers, where he was in charge of building dams in Oregon and Montana.

Helm Kee Chinn and his father were also among the earliest families to move outside of Chinatown into a residential neighborhood. Sometime around 1920, they purchased two houses, side by side, on 17th Avenue not too far from Chinatown. Several years earlier, Mar Dong, who arrived here from San Francisco in 1907 and quickly established himself as a successful businessman, bought a house on 29th Avenue in what is now called the Central Area. His family was probably the first Chinese family to move out of Chinatown. At that time, the Central Area was predominately white working class, an area occupied by Jews and many synagogues.

By 1940, about 40 Chinese families had moved into the Central Area. The neighborhood was a natural progression away from the nearby Chinatown area. Chinese and Japanese also began moving to the North Beacon Hill area, another neighborhood close to the International District. Other areas of the city were closed to Asians and other non-whites because of covenants restricting the sale of homes to non-whites.

The residential mobility of Asians in Seattle, particularly the Chinese, was also limited because many were men who were either sojourners, single, or married with families back in their home country. Rather than move outside the International District and pay more for housing and face the hostility of whites, they remained to enjoy what little comfort and conveniences they had.

Part Seven
Japanese American Removal and Incarceration

The Seeds of Anti-Japanese American Hostility

On December 7, 1941, Japan attacked Pearl Harbor. Within a few months, over 120,000 Japanese Americans on the West Coast - citizens and aliens, elderly and infants, men and women, students and professionals, farmers and clerks - were forced to leave their homes and imprisoned in concentration camps, not for military reasons, but because of racial prejudice. Far from an isolated incident, this incarceration was the culmination of years of racial hostility against Japanese Americans.

With the passage of the 1882 Chinese Exclusion Act, many white Americans thought they had stemmed the flow of Asians into the United States. But as the number of Japanese immigrants grew, the hostility and racism previously directed at the Chinese shifted to the Japanese. Like the Chinese before them, the Japanese were perceived as unfair labor competition, immoral and unassimilable because they were not white. Antagonism toward the Japanese was at first sporadic, and concentrated in California. Labor leaders and demagogic politicians led the anti-Japanese movement. As early as 1888, when there were still only a few Japanese in the U.S., the San Francisco Trades Council called attention to a "recently developed phase of the Mongolian issue."

Four years later, the infamous Dennis Kearney, a leader in the anti-Chinese movement, told the public about "another horde of Asiatic slaves" filling the gap "made vacant by the Chinese." "We are paying out our money," he said, so that "fully developed men who know no morals by vice [may] sit beside our daughters to debauch [and] demoralize them. The Japs must go." The San Francisco School Board, on June 14, 1893, passed a resolution requiring that "all persons of the Japanese race seeking entrance to the public schools must attend what is known as the Chinese School." The Chinese School was a segregated school established by the Board. After some protests by the Japanese, including a plea in person by the Japanese Consul, the Board reversed its decision.

At the turn of the century, hostility toward the Japanese increased. The San Francisco Building Trades Council, on April 12, 1900, passed a resolution that read in part:

...the present open-door policy toward Japanese immigrants is injurious to labor and detrimental to the best interest of the country...We respectfully petition our Senators and Representatives in Congress to use their best efforts to enact a similar law [to the Chinese Exclusion Act] or secure such international agreement as will secure this Coast against any further Japanese immigration, [and] thus forever settle the rooted Mongolian labor problem.

A month later, San Francisco Mayor James D. Phelan, at a meeting called by various labor unions, said: "The Japanese are starting the same tide of immigration which we thought had been checked twenty years ago. The Chinese and Japanese are not bona fide citizens. They are not the stuff of which American citizens can be made."

In Washington, the local Western Central Labor Union passed resolutions denouncing Japanese immigration. The sentiments of labor quickly spread to the political arena, and the King County Republican Club approved similar resolutions petitioning Congress to pass a Japanese Exclusion Act. State delegates to the National Republican Consortium decided they should "use every effort to secure the insertion of an anti-Japanese clause in the National Republican Platform." The McKinley Republican Club, a local group, passed yet another set of resolutions, which read in part:

Whereas during the first few months a large number of Japanese laborers have migrated or have been imported to the Pacific Coast of the United States...

Whereas, said laborers consist of a class who live and subsist at so small a cost that they unfairly enter directly into competition with intelligent American workmen...

Whereas, said Japanese laborers are a menace to the conditions which make it possible for the intelligent American workingman

Development of Yesler Terrace Project cuts off portion of the District

Yesler Terrace is a public housing project, constructed and operated by the Seattle Housing Authority in the early 1940s. When it was initially built, it contained some 600 low-rise housing units and housed over 1200 persons. Commonly known as the "projects," the Terrace is located adjacent to the International District and downtown, on a hilltop in a highly desirable location. In earlier days, the area was called "Profanity Hill" because the city's courthouse was situated near the this steep incline, and the lawyers and judges cursed because the cable cars frequently malfunctioned, forcing them to climb the hill.

The southern portion of Yesler Terrace (south of Yesler Way) was occupied by a racially-mixed population prior to its construction. Some one thousand residents - 42% white, 33% Japanese and the rest Filipinos,

Yesler Terrace. International Examiner file photo.

Chinese, Hawaiians, and Blacks- were displaced to make way for the project.[1] Some 18 prostitution houses, a grocery store, a Chinese laundry, and two Japanese-operated

hotels also had to be demolished as were three Japanese churches, including the Shinto Temple and Buddhist Church.

Conveniently located next to downtown and the International District with commanding views of the downtown skyline and Elliott Bay, the Yesler Terrace was the first racially-integrated housing project in the country. Victor Steinbrueck, who later led the campaign to save the Pike Place Market, was the architect for the residential community. The European style of both the residential units' design and the layout of the community, as well as the low-medium scale of the entire project, now makes Yesler Terrace appear much like middle income housing rather than low-income housing.

1. Irene Miller, *Profanity Hill*, The Working Press, Everett, Washington, 1979. pp. 1 and 2

---

to maintain himself, his family and his home...

Whereas, the immigration and importation of said Japanese laborers to the Pacific Coast will speedily produce the conditions which now exist in southern states, with all of is race controversies and race horrors...

Resolved, that the further importation and immigration of said Japanese should be limited and restricted...

Resolved, that the act of Congress entitled, 'An act to prohibit the coming of Chinese laborers to the United States should be amended by inserting the words 'and Japanese' after the word 'Chinese'...

Resolved, that a copy of these resolutions be forthwith transmitted...to all senators and member of Congress...

Resolved, that all Republican newspapers be requested to publish these resolutions.

Even though there was a need for additional laborers in the state, it was clear that many wanted Washington preserved for whites. The racial tolerance of Washingtonians dwindled as visions of a state with mixed races and cultures instilled fears of another South. Racial harmony

was not on the agenda; getting rid of Asians was.

Racism in Organized Labor

In 1905, California labor unions joined forces to start the Asiatic Exclusion League. Four union bosses, all immigrants, were primarily responsible for starting the league: Patrick McCarthy (from Ireland), chief of the San Francisco Building Trades Council; his assistant, Olaf Tveitmore (from Sweden); and two representatives of the Sailors' Union, Walter MacArthur (from Scotland) and Andrew Furuseth (from Norway). The League sought not only to stop all Japanese immigration, but also to impede the right of Asians to earn a livelihood. Furuseth, for instance, wanted a law forcing Asian seamen off American ships; the power of the white race, he claimed, rested on its control of the seas. Hiring Asian seamen instead of whites threatened that control.

One staunch leader of the anti-Japanese forces was Samuel Gompers, founder of the American Federation of Labor (AFL).[1] Gompers himself was a Jewish immigrant who, early in life, embraced the ideals of brotherhood and class solidarity, but later repudiated those ideals and became one of organized labor's most tenacious advocates of white racial superiority. Expressing the view of many in organized labor, Gompers persistently urged an end to Asian immigration and exclusion of non-whites from unions, asserting that a person had to be white to be American. Having earlier played a leading role in the passage of the Chinese Exclusion Act, Gompers now turned his attention to the Japanese. He once went so as far as to say that "maintenance of the nation depend[ed] upon maintenance of racial purity," and that it was not in the nation's interest to allow "cheap labor that could not be Americanized and could not be taught to render the same intelligent efficient service as was supplied by American workers." On several occasions, Gompers refused to grant AFL charters to unions with Japanese members.

After the 1906 San Francisco earthquake, the city's school board passed another segregation order, requiring all Japanese and Korean children to attend segregated schools in Chinatown. The Japanese government became infuriated and protested the decision to the White House. President Theodore Roosevelt, after meeting with a delegation from California, persuaded the school board to rescind its order after promising to limit Japanese immigration. Meanwhile, in Vancouver, B.C., a parade and mass meeting sponsored by the Asiatic Exclusion

Evacuation of Japanese Americans from the West Coast. Library of Congress photo.

League turned into a race riot. On September 17, 1907, a mob that grew to 30,000 stormed Chinatown and then proceeded to the Japanese quarters. The Japanese bravely fought back their attackers, who wanted an end to Japanese immigration. Shortly after the riot, the London Times reported that American agitators had instigated the violence. Named were Frank Cotterill, Washington Federation of Labor president; A.E. Fowler, secretary of the Japanese Exclusion League of Seattle; and A.P. Listman, a prominent Seattle labor leader.

Eighteen months of negotiation between Japan and the United States ended with the infamous Gentlemen's Agreement. Japan agreed to continue its policy of discouraging immigration. Passports to the United States would be issued only to "non-laborers or [those] who, in coming to the continent, seek to resume a formerly acquired domicile to join parent, wife or children residing there, or to assume active control of an already possessed interest in a farming enterprise in this country." While the Agreement may have helped families to develop and encourage Japanese settlement in the U.S., it dramatically reduced Japanese immigration to America. "The whole object nominally desired by those who wish to prevent the incoming of Japanese laborers has been achieved," wrote President Teddy Roosevelt. Ironically, more Japanese were leaving the United States at the time than entering. An observer noted that "by present indications, in a very few years the number of Japanese there will be no greater than the number of Americans in Japan."

Although organized labor and others had succeeded in cutting off the immigration of Japanese laborers, they did not stop there. The focus shifted from laborers to "picture brides" and even the wives of residents, although the latter were permitted entry under the Agreement. The vision of hordes of Japanese invading Western America, the "Yellow Peril," resurfaced again and again.

Racism in the Law

Meanwhile, anti-Japanese forces increased their efforts to restrict the right of Japanese Americans to a livelihood. As aliens, Japanese were barred from full participation in the legal system and from the privileges of citizenship. In 1894, a Japanese named Saito applied for citizenship in Massachusetts. Saito was the first Asian alien to challenge America's naturalization laws. The laws regarding naturalization were originally passed in 1790 and decreed that any alien, "free white person" who has resided in the United States for a certain stated time could become a citizen. In 1873, the naturalization law was revised to include "American blacks" and "persons of African nativity or descent." Saito argued that he fit within the category of "a free white person." A Massachusetts court rejected his contention, stating that the races of mankind are "white, black, brown and yellow." Since Saito belonged to the "yellow" race, he was ineligible for citizenship. The court pointed out that the earliest naturalization laws were originally intended to extend citizenship only to members of the Caucasian race. That specific revisions were made to include blacks bolstered the court's belief that the yellow race was to be excluded from the privilege of applying for citizenship.

Washington State courts originally admitted Japanese petitions for naturalization, but these petitions were overruled by the U. S. Supreme Court. In Yamashita vs. Hinkley, the Supreme Court overturned a Washington state court decision granting Yamashita's application for citizenship. The Superior Court had issued Yamashita a certificate of naturalization. He then tried to create a corporation, but state law prohibited non-citizens from doing so. When he filed his corporation papers, Washington's Secretary of State refused to accept them on the basis that Yamashita was ineligible for citizenship because he was not a free white man. The case went to the U. S. Supreme Court, which held that the Superior Court of Washington had no power to confer citizenship. On November 13, 1922, the same day as the Yamashita decision, the Supreme Court closed the doors to Japanese naturalization in Ozawa v. United States. The Court ruled that Ozawa was "clearly of a race which is not Caucasian, and therefore belong[ed] entirely outside the zone on the negative side."

The law also prevented Japanese Americans from owning land. California passed the first Alien Land Law in 1913. The original California law denied all persons ineligible for citizenship the right to own or lease land. In deference to white landowners, however, it was amended to permit leasing for no more than three years. In 1921, Washington State passed an Alien Land Law, after California had strengthened its own law. This time, the anti-Japanese forces were joined by the newly formed American Legion and the Native Sons and Daughters of the Golden West.

During World War I, when Japan was an ally of the U. S., there was more tolerance for Japanese in America. However, with the return of veterans and a national recession, anti-Japanese agitation resurfaced and the anti-Japanese exclusionists achieved victory. The Immigration Act of 1924 effectively stopped entry of Japanese to the United States. With the curtailment of Japanese immigration and the gradual societal acceptance of second-generation Japanese, blatant acts of anti-Japanese racism cooled during the 1930s. However, by World War II, animosities, vicious stereotypes, and discrimination against the Japanese increased.

The Incarceration

The attack on Pearl Harbor and the war with Japan rekindled and heightened the animosity against Japanese Americans. The public and political outcry quickly turned into an official policy of evacuation. On February 19, 1942, President Franklin Roosevelt signed Executive Order 9066, which authorized any military commander to evacuate any person of Japanese ancestry from the West Coast. Japanese Americans on the West Coast, more than two-thirds of them U.S. citizens, were ordered to leave their homes and businesses. "The Japanese race is an enemy race and while many second and third generation Japanese born on United States soil, possessed of United States citizenship, have become Americanized, the strains are undiluted," said General J.L. DeWitt, Western Defense Commander.

Some who were community leaders were arrested without warrants and held without indictment or statement of charges. The rest were first transported to hastily constructed assembly centers and then to more permanent concentration camps in desolate, inland areas. So-called measures to protect the Japanese from the forced sale of their property were wholly ineffective; evacuation re-

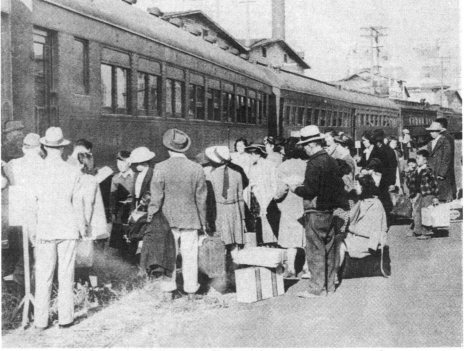

Japanese Americans departing from Seattle for Puyallup.

sulted in financial disaster, torment and hardships for virtually every family. Most of the Japanese in the Puget Sound area were shipped like cattle to an assembly area at what is now the Puyallup Fairgrounds, and then to Minidoka, Idaho.

Masao Takahashi was a cannery foreman prior to World War II. Married, with a wife and five children, he was a caring father and sole provider for the family. He was also one of the leaders in the community. His testimony before the U. S. Commission on Wartime Relocation and Internment of Civilians recounted the hardships and trauma of evacuation: "On the very day of my eldest daughter's eleventh birthday, February 21, 1942, I was roused from my sleep very early in the morning. The FBI, along with four Seattle policemen, searched my house, ransack-

ing closets. I was allowed to dress, but under observation, even in my morning toiletry.

"I was placed in the Immigration Detention Center. Apparently, I was part of the second group of men to be taken by authorities...I recall feeling confident that I would be released in time to eat birthday cake with my family that evening. However, when we were stripped naked and thoroughly inspected, my optimism was shaken by the very humiliation of the process. I assumed that cooperation would lead to an early release and resolved to accept the inevitable.

"But that was not to be. The days were added on to days. Tense boredom, terrible food, and wild rumors were our daily preoccupation... From the window of the Detention Center, I could see our house...I remember a friendly guard teased my visiting five-year-old daughter by slamming the barred gates closed and telling her she was now a captive. She flew into my arms joyfully, saying, 'Oh, boy, now I can stay with papa.' Mama had tears in her eyes and I wished I could cry, too."

Takahashi testified that, after about a month and a half, he was transferred to Missoula, Montana: "I was allowed a few minutes to walk to the fence to say goodbye to them. I was at a loss to find comforting words. Boarding the train, I heard my daughters crying out, 'Papa, papa.' I can not describe how I felt at the time. I can still hear the ring of their crying in my ears today. This was the first time it occurred to me that I might not see them again...

"From somewhere in Louisiana, I wound up in a camp in New Mexico. It seems I was kept constantly on the move with little rhyme or reason. It was from this camp in Santa Fe that I was able to make arrangements to go to Crystal City, Texas where I would be reunited with my family. My numb feelings were revitalized. I had tried to imagine what their lives were like since their incarceration..."

Takahashi's eldest daughter, Kazzie

Katayama, recalls her feelings about returning to Seattle after the war: "Seattle looked strange for a long time after we returned here...I had never noticed before the hostility on the faces of many Seattle residents. My father's former position as a cannery foreman was closed to him. Undaunted, he was determined to rebuild his life, and my mother was solidly behind him. So were the children... My parents were never to regain the prominence and economic security that they had prior to World War II."

Katayama also describes the daily frustrations and humiliation the Japanese typi-

Higo's 10¢ Store on Jackson Street during the war. Wing Luke Asian Museum photo.

cally experienced: "My mother had the comb and ribbons I had picked out in her hand along with the five dollar bill. It was obvious the Woolworth saleslady was not going to wait on us. I was mad and told mom I didn't

want that 'junk' anymore. But mama wouldn't listen. She kept on staring at the lady who was pretending to be busy. I ended up madder at mama than the saleslady. When she finally rang up our sale, she was very rude, but I was more relieved it was over and chagrined that mama could be so stubborn...

"Another time, mama and I were at the fish market. She had asked for several fish heads. The market man bluntly told her she would have to pay for the heads. I flushed with embarrassment because I knew mama had intended to get it free. She lied when she said, 'Of course,' and pointed to the man. Going places with mama had become increasingly difficult for me."

Most of the Japanese who returned to Seattle had lost their jobs, homes, investments, savings and business. They faced the prospect of beginning anew when they came back, without financial resources, in a city full of people who considered them an enemy race. Some, like George Tokuda, a druggist, reestablished their businesses, but at a price. Tokuda had been forced to sell his business during the war at 10 percent of its actual value. With borrowed money, he started a new drugstore after the war, near the site of his previous store. In a short time, he was able to buy back his previous store; the owners had lost business because they refused to serve Japanese patrons.

Part Eight
International District Emerges After World War II

Chinese Americans Move into Mainstream

For Chinese Americans in Seattle, World War II marked a new chapter. The turning point came when Japanese planes bombed Pearl Harbor and the United States became allies with China in the war against Japan. When twin boys were born to Dick Chin (a waiter at King Nam Cafe) and his wife Annie - just three months after the U.S. declared war - the Seattle Times published a picture of the mother and twins with the headline, "Chinese Start Right." The caption read, "Training starts early for Chinese children these wartime days," noting that "China" buttons were pinned on the twins' blanket at age two.

For the first time, Chinese Americans were able to enter the mainstream work force and earn decent wages. Labor was badly needed, especially in the defense industry and with companies like Boeing and Todd Shipyard. Those who could speak English - even a little - signed up as riveters, janitors, mechanics' helpers, secretaries, or draftsmen. Others were drafted into the armed forces and assigned technical work. Although many older immigrant bachelors remained at jobs in Chinatown, younger Chinese Americans took over stores and shops left behind by Japanese Americans who were imprisoned during the war.

In 1943, President Franklin D. Roosevelt signed an act repealing the earlier Chinese Exclusion Acts. Washington Senator Warren G. Magnuson sponsored this act at the urging of local Chinese Americans. The new law established an annual quota of 105 Chinese immigrants to the United States and allowed Chinese to become naturalized citizens. Those who became citizens could then apply to have their wives come over from China or Hong Kong. Four years later, the War Brides Act was amended to allow wives of Chinese American servicemen to enter the United States on a non-quota basis. Consequently, a number of Chinese American servicemen went to China or Hong Kong and returned with brides.

The net result of the Magnuson and War Brides Acts was the migration of nearly 2,000 Chinese (mostly immigrants) to Washington State between World War II and 1960. More importantly, the new laws led to a substantial increase in wives and the formation of families. From 1940 to 1960, there were some 1,900 Chinese American births in Washington, much more than in previous years. From 1940 to 1950, the Chinese American population in Seattle increased from 1,781 to 2,650. By 1960, the number had jumped 65 percent to 4,176. By this time, four-fifths of all Chinese in the state lived in Seattle.

The second generation Chinese Americans clearly benefited from the events of World War II. The war offered this second generation a crack in the walls of discrimination, a chance to improve their economic status. They jumped at the opportunity. According to the 1940 census, only 2.5 percent of the Chinese male work force were professionals or technical workers. Ten years later, that figure was 9.5 percent. By 1960, it jumped to 25.5 percent - by far the largest occupational grouping among Chinese males. During this same period, the percentage of Chinese males in the managerial/proprietor occupational grouping fell from 23 percent in 1940 and 25.5 percent in 1950 to 16 percent in 1960. The percentage of waiters and laundry workers also dropped substantially from 1940 to 1960.

To say that Chinese were prepared for professional and technical work is an understatement. In 1940, when educational attainment would not have helped Chinese get better jobs, only 2.5 percent of the Chinese in the state were college graduates, compared to 6 percent for whites. A decade later, the Chinese percentage was 10.2 percent, surpassing the white percentage of 8. By 1960, the percentage of Chinese college graduates was 18 percent, twice as high as for whites.

The second generation's subculture included American cultural institutions set up exclusively for Chinese. In 1923, Boy Scout

'For haircuts, this is the place!' (excerpted)

(Lisa Kinoshita, *International Examiner*, January 15-February 15, 1981)

Few people today associate hairstyling with the International District. But 40 years ago, shears in more than 30 barber shops clipped feverishly, and competitively, to serve customers whose visits were as much an excuse for chatting with friends as for getting a trim...[T]he tradition...lives on in shops like Bob Sakoda's (Bob's) and Florencio Della's Liberty....Neatly smocked barbers of the old school, they pride themselves on their mastery of a few basic cuts practiced for years on regular customers....When the shops first opened...a shave and a haircut were, as the song goes, "four bits" (fifty cents).

Della works part-time in the shop at 506 Maynard Avenue South. Behind the single barber's chair, finishing a cut on Vincent Mendoza, a customer of 15 years, the diminutive Della stood barely half a head taller than his seated friend.

Mendoza...declared, "For haircuts, this is the place!"

...Della describes the Liberty as an "international barbershop," where he grooms "every kind of head." But, he adds, "Birds of a feather flock together...because I'm a Filipino many Filipinos come around here."

Della arrived from the Philippines in 1927. Before becoming a full-time barber in 1950, he worked summers in Alaska, and held other jobs the rest of the year, including work in the shipyards.

In 1937, Della went to the Moller barber school in Los Angeles for one year. After the war he was laid off from the shipyards, and he turned to barbering as part-time work alternating with working in Alaska in the summers.

He spoke of those early days affectionately: "In Alaska time, there used to be a lot of people here [some I.D. hotels were packed with Filipinos]. They'd come down and play music."

...Each winter presented problems because his "Filipino friends [would] run off to California to work at the canneries...they come back in June." Thus winter was a slow season for Della.

...Della is proud of the Liberty barbershop as a special place where senior citizens could visit...to play solitaire by the window, talk, watch one of the two televisions stacked against the wall, or just sit....On the pale aquamarine walls of the Liberty are aged black and white pictures of haircuts with names like "Flair Ivy," "Zodiac," "Smooth Edwardian," and "Feathered edged neckline." Prices range from $3.50 for children's cuts to $4.75 for long hair....

Bob Sakoda's barbershop is practically a monument in the I.D. For almost 60 years the Sakodas, first Ittoku (Bob's father), and now Bob, have worked out of the busy, two chair shop on Weller Street between Sixth and Maynard....[Both] Ittoku and wife Mine...were professional barbers from Japan who underwent professional apprenticeships, which meant free room and board from the teacher, and "working for almost nothing."

Ittoku bought a Chinese laundry with a boiler in back and converted it into the barbershop in 1920 or 1921. Sakoda remembers the heyday of Filipino and Japanese haircutters, when "every block had a barbershop."

Even with thick competition, [Bob] says that his father's business thrived....In grade school Ittoku gave him $1 a week allowance. "That's a lot of money during that time," he laughed.

International Examiner file photo.

Pointing out some small side rooms in the shop, he explained that in the early 1930s they were baths. Single rooms in the old hotels didn't have baths...so people would come down to his barbershop and bathe for 25 cents.

When World War II began, Ittoku Sakoda had to do something with the business before entering the concentration camp at Minidoka, Idaho, with his family.

"My father sold the shop to an Italian for $500 in 1941," said Sakoda. The Italian man, another barber, after the war sold the shop back to Ittoku for $500.

After release from Minidoka, jobs were scarce; perhaps more so for Bob Sakoda because of racial prejudice. After several jobs ranging from dishwasher to "soda jerk," he finally turned to barbering, and took a year of schooling at Moler's.

"...I wasn't too enthused [about barbering], but it seemed the quickest way to make some money and support my family." A second later the laughter comes. "I'm still at it," he chuckles.

Bob joined his father's business, and took over when Ittoku retired in the 1960s...The demand for specialized skills in cutting Asian hair eventually resulted in an overflow of clients. Many went elsewhere for haircuts; then, unhappy with the results, returned.

Time-consuming details in Sakoda's work include cleaning out the ears with a small, sharp knife...and shaping the eyebrows with a razor....

But perhaps the biggest reward Sakoda gets from barbering is not monetary. He enjoys the friendships formed over the years, which made him a well-known figure in the I.D. "Walk down Chinatown with me, I have to raise hands every other minute [to wave]...That's how long I've been here."

Troop 54 was established (a Girl Scout troop was formed in 1940). A Chinese art club that included Fay Chong and Andrew Chinn (both noted watercolor artists) was founded in Chinatown in 1937. After World War II, a Chinese American veterans group was born, the Cathay Post #186 of the American Legion, as were the Miss Chinatown pageant and the Chinatown Chamber of Commerce. Chinese student clubs were formed in high schools and colleges. The organization that received the most acclaim was the Chinese Community Girls Drill Team, founded by restaurateur Ruby Chow and others in 1952. The team traveled throughout the United States and abroad and won numerous awards.

Some Chinese were able to accumulate enough savings and, with financial help from relatives, started small businesses. These first generation immigrants, some of whom had been in the city for years, typically purchased small, family-operated restaurants or grocery stores in the late 1940s and early 50s. These businesses demanded long work hours, which the family could provide, and a limited amount of capital and technical skills for successful operation. A family couldn't get rich from these businesses, but they could make enough to survive comfortably.

Many first generation women worked in the garment or laundry business, since the ability to speak English was not required there. Black Bear Manufactory, on Rainier Avenue, was one of the larger employers of Chinese garment workers. A commercial laundry on Twelfth Avenue, between Yesler Way and Fir Street, employed a large number of Chinese women. Meanwhile, the immigrant bachelor society in Chinatown had slowly declined.

While some had returned to China or moved elsewhere, others still harbored hopes of returning to their home villages. Those hopes ended with China's Communist revolution in 1949. The era of the Chinese sojourners was over.

With the newly created alliance between China and the United States, the American attitude toward the Chinese in America began to shift. For the first time, substantial numbers of Chinese were permitted to live in parts of the city outside Chinatown. Chinese were recruited or drafted to work in the defense industries in the region. The result was a rise in the per capita income of Chinese Americans and a decline in the Chinese population in Chinatown. "There were about a hundred Chinese families back then before World War II, and maybe a hundred Japanese families," said Ben Woo, who grew up in the District before the war years and later became a leader in the revitalization of the area. "That's just a ballpark figure. It was like a little village."[1] But by the 1950s, most Chinese still in Chinatown were part of the bachelor society; few families remained in the area. During the late 1940s and 50s, many Chinese had purchased houses in the Central Area and on Beacon Hill. By 1960, there were a considerable number of Chinese residents in North Beacon Hill, even more than in the Central Area.

In spite of the mass migration out of Chinatown, Dr. Henry Luke, a family physician for much of the Chinese community, kept his office at a run-down house on Seventh Avenue, next to Chong Wa Benevolent Association play field. Like Dr. Luke's office, the buildings in the Chinatown core and the surrounding area had become run-down. The hotel and association buildings showed the wear of age and deferred maintenance. Residents lived in small substan-

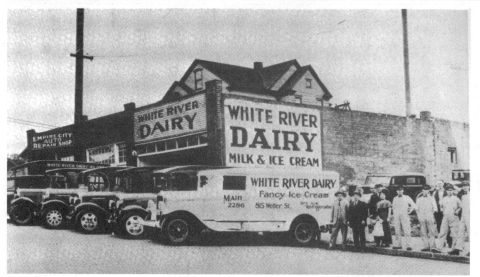

White River Dairy. Shigako Uno photo.

dard rooms that lacked heating, had inadequate plumbing, chipped and cracked paint and rodent problems. With few exceptions, the buildings in Chinatown had not been upgraded since they were first erected. Behind such successful restaurants as Tai Tung, Hong Kong, Eight Immortals, Linyen and others was a rapidly declining Chinatown that had become a blighted slum.

The Decline of Japantown

"When the Japanese began to return in January 1945," wrote Howard Droker, "Seattle confronted its gravest racial problem. Although the blind racism and fear that were largely responsible for the evacuation of the Japanese had abated to some degree, self-styled 'patriotic' anti-Japanese groups had formed. These, together with certain economic groups, were opposed to the move back to the West Coast. But a public sense of guilt, the efforts of civic groups, and the favorable publicity given to the Japanese-

American soldiers by the federal government helped to lessen racial tensions and ease the return".[2]

Seattle's mayor at end of the war, William F. Devin, originally joined the mayors of several large cities on the West Coast in opposing the return of Japanese Americans

---

The Japanese in Seattle prior to World War II totaled nearly 7,000. After the war, the number dropped to some 4,700.

---

to the coast. However, once the government decided to allow them back, the conservative mayor left the matter to his Civic Unity Committee. Mayor Devin had established the committee earlier to ease racial tensions

in the city and to make recommendations to avoid outbreaks of violence in the wake of race riots that had occurred in Detroit, Harlem and Los Angeles. Citing the sacrifices and heroism of Japanese American soldiers in Europe and the Pacific, the multiracial committee passed a resolution hoping "that Seattle will respond as a truly American city and grant the returning American-Japanese citizens all the rights to which they are legally entitled."

Washington Governor Mon Wallgren also disapproved of the return of Japanese Americans, as did the Japanese Exclusion League and the Remember Pearl Harbor League. Veterans groups sided with the Army's wishes for the return of the Japanese, but many labor unions feared renewed labor competition. The Washington Teamsters and their leader, Dave Beck, were very vocal in their opposition. Produce dealers and farmers, especially in the Kent Valley, were another element opposed to the return of the Japanese.

"After the war, Japantown was no longer there," said Shigeko Uno, who was born in the District. Uno's parents owned and operated the White River Dairy on Weller Street but lost it when they were sent to camp. "Even the Japanese people who came back and started their businesses," she says, "their children didn't want to continue, so there's the end of it. We started Chick's Ice Creamery on Jackson Street underneath the Bush Hotel from 1947 to 1960. During the early years it was fun because people would be coming back from all over and they would all gather at our place. Everybody would be so happy to see each other."[3]

The Japanese in Seattle prior to World War II totaled nearly 7,000. After the war, the number dropped to some 4,700. It was estimated that 65-70 percent of Seattle's interned Japanese later returned to the city. Prior to World War II, the Japanese in the city operated 206 hotels, 140 groceries, 94 cleaning establishments, 64 market stands, and 57 wholesale produce houses, according to a survey prepared by the Japanese American Citizens League.[4] Except for the hotel operators, there were only a few groceries, restaurants, and produce market stands in the District after the war. Most of the Japanese businesses in the District that existed prior to the war never restarted. Many were hastily sold before evacuation. Those that did start new were relatively small and dependent on the trade of the Japanese community or other minorities in the immediate area for business. Largely dependent upon a white clientele, the Japanese produce business never again reached the heights it had achieved before the war.

The Jackson Street Community Council

The population in the International District grew to 4,800 in 1950, compared to 3,733 in 1940. This 30 percent increase reflects the heavy migration to Seattle of workers who found jobs in wartime industries. Included in this migration were African Americans, some of whom settled in the District and opened businesses along Jackson Street, including a pharmacy, a large nightclub, several restaurants and taverns, tailor shops and cleaners. By the end of the decade, Blacks had become the largest racial minority in Seattle. Subsequently, the racial antagonism directed at Asians shifted more to African Americans.

One of the top nightclubs in the District, Basin Street, opened in 1940 when Davey Lee, a local businessman, won a stake playing the Chinese lottery.[5] At 17, local jazz great Ernestine Anderson began her professional

A young Ray Charles, left, got his first paid gig at the Black Elks Club in the International District in 1947.

career at the club singing with the Ernie Lewis band. The club was on Maynard Avenue, off Jackson Street, in a basement that extended from the Bush Hotel to an area underneath what is now Hing Hay Park.[6] It held about 200 patrons and had some 20 full-time waiters and five bartenders. Paul de Barros describes the scene at the Basin Street during its heyday:

The music began at noon with a single pianist, graduated to trios at three, and a four-piece band at nine, followed by the main attraction - the Ernie Lewis band - at 1 a.m. The after-hours set lasted all night, six nights a week. Every once in a while, out-of-town acts came in, including the Ink spots, Dexter Gordon, the great tap dancer Teddy Hale, and Sammy Davis, Jr., who at the time was work-ing with his uncle's vaudeville group, the Will Mastin Trio. Jabo Ward considered Basin Street one of the two or three places where, musically, players felt they could let their hair down. Floor shows with chorus girls and exotic dancing were a specialty, including a drag act in which one dancer flung another around by the hair....

In 1946, a multiracial organization, sponsored by the United Good Neighborhood (forerunner to the United Way of King County), was formed. The Jackson Street Community Council, a grassroots self-help group, sought to improve the declining physical/social conditions and create racial harmony within the area from Fourth Avenue to Twenty-third Avenue along Jackson Street. This area included what is now considered the International District as well as the neighborhoods east of it; these neighborhoods comprised a racially mixed area of blacks, Chinese, Japanese, Filipinos and whites. The area was Seattle's racial ghetto and the District was quickly becoming a slum.

The Council, which was relatively successful and served as a model for other community organizations, lasted some 20 years as a separate entity. Governed by a 15-member board, the Council was the first neighborhood revitalization organization in the city established to improve social, economic, and physical conditions. United Good Neighborhood funds were used to pay for staff and administrative costs. Ruth Manca served as its Executive Director from 1946 to 1955. Much of its work was done in concert with city officials and administrators, who regularly appeared at council meetings. Phil Hayasaka was the Council's Executive Director in the 1960s and later became director of the city's Human Rights Department. In 1967, under the leadership of Ruth Brandwein, the Jackson Street Community Council merged with the Central Area Community Council to become the Central Seattle Community Council. In 1971, the Council became the Seattle-King County Community Council Federation. Don Chinn, Ruth Chinn, Lew Kay, James Matsuoka, Clarence Arai, Victor Velasco, Tad Yamaguchi, Rev. P.J. Daba, Juan Castillo, Val Laigo, Ben Woo, James Mar, Tak Kubota and Fred Cordova were among those who were actively involved with the Jackson Street Council at one time or another during its history.

The council was effective in initiating and organizing cleanup campaigns, voter registration drives, and naturalization programs. It was a watchdog that worked to eliminate prostitution and was soundly critical of the police for being lax towards such activity in the area. It sponsored chest X-ray campaigns to detect tuberculosis and published posters and leaflets in Chinese, Japanese and English to promote the campaigns. Its successes ranged from clearing and improving vacant lots and bettering health care, to planting trees on the hillside below Yesler Terrace and building a retaining wall along Jackson Street, to getting streets paved and improving street lighting. Perhaps the Jackson Street Community Council's most notable achievement was getting the state legislature to allow "urban renewal areas" and getting the Yesler/Atlantic neighborhood designated as such in 1959 so that it could receive federal funds and assistance for neighborhood improvements.

Because the area was multiracial - with immigrants from many different countries - Jackson Street Council members, elected city officials and others referred to the entire area as the International Area, International Settlement or International Center in the latter 1940s, after World War II. The designation of the area as the International District originates from this usage. The Jackson Street Council sponsored events which also used the term "International," such as its annual International Festival and International Queen Contest. In 1952, Mayor Devin, after recommending an extension of a city curfew requested by Chinese businessmen, officially proclaimed the area as the "International Center." The designation covered the area from Fourth to Fourteenth Avenues and Yesler Way to Dearborn Street. The mayor noted that it was a tourist attraction area, and that the area's Chinese, Japanese, Filipino, and African Americans made outstanding contributions to the cultural and civic life of the city.[7]

In the 1950s, a spin-off group made up of businesspersons called the International Improvement Association established an annual citywide cultural and entertainment program to show the importance of contributions of the people in the area. Consequently, the "International Festival" was initially held on Main Street and Sixth Avenue during the summer and eventually became part of Seattle Seafair. Another event, the International Art Exhibit, included such well-known artists as George Tsutakawa, Fay Chong and James Washington, Jr. The group also started an annual International Queen Contest, organized by Ann Wing. Four different queens were chosen, representing the Chinese, Filipino, Japanese and African American sectors respectively.

Housing was another issue in which the Jackson Street Council was in the vanguard. Much of the housing in the International District was owned by absentee landlords who did little, if anything, to maintain their properties. The Jackson Street Council lobbied the city to pass a minimum housing code ordinance to increase the supply of safe and decent housing in the District. It was the first housing ordinance of its kind in the city and an important method to have property owners in the area to renovate and maintain their structures.

However, the Jackson Street Council was unable to prevent construction of the Interstate 5 freeway through the District. City planners had proposed a viaduct from Dearborn Avenue to Yesler Way over Eighth Avenue as early as 1948. Construction of a viaduct or a freeway through there, the Council feared, would divide the District in half. In 1965, when the Seattle portion of Interstate 5 was completed, the fears of the Council became reality.

Part Nine
The District Battles Hard Times

Problems in the District Deepen

In 1960, after years of selling insurance, Robert Chinn started United Savings and Loan - the first Chinese American savings and loan in America - at the corner of the Bush Hotel complex with just a couple of teller windows. That same year, Han Chinn opened the Four Seas Restaurant at the northwest corner of Eighth Avenue and King Street, the first new building in years and the first restaurant with parking on the same lot. Such developments would normally suggest good times for the District, and indeed, the Four Seas quickly became the rave among area restaurants. However, the Safeway supermarket immediately north of it closed, signaling the neighborhood's declining residential population base.

By this time, a frustrated group of mostly American-born Chinese professionals started the Chinese Community Service Organization (CCSO), in an attempt to get Chong Wa Benevolent Association to change. As in the past, mostly foreign-born, elderly businessmen controlled Chong Wa, clinging to what many younger members considered the "old Chinese way of thinking and doing things." The leaders of Chong Wa, said one CCSO member, "were oriented too much towards old China and the old Chinese ways. Too old-fashioned. We wanted Chong Wa to change and to address the issues facing the Chinese people here."

Around the same time, Don Chin, a local merchant active in the Jackson Street Community Council and Chong Wa (who later directed Inter*Im), started the Chinatown Chamber of Commerce, a small group of Chinese merchants who wanted to promote business in the area. The Chamber sponsored promotional events during Chinese New Year and Seafair. Both CCSO and the Chamber had membership in Chong Wa, but their emergence suggests Chong Wa's failure to incorporate certain concerns and interests in the Chinese community.

Wing Luke, who later became the first Asian American elected to the Seattle City Council, was one of those who started CCSO. Perhaps if Luke had used his influence on the City Council to enhance the goals of CCSO, it might have become a real base of power in the District and the greater Chinese community. However, he never actively participated in the organization despite being its first president, and CCSO never had very much influence. After he died in an airplane crash, his friends founded the Wing Luke Asian Museum, which became the main cultural center in the International District. Perhaps CCSO's greatest achievement was obtaining money for putting up Chinese lanterns in Chinatown, in 1962.

When Seattle's Model Cities Program arrived in 1968, the boundaries of the District were established (roughly from Fifth to Twelfth Avenues South and Yesler Way to Dearborn Streets, excluding the Yesler Terrace neighborhood), and Chinatown was effectively incorporated into a broader jurisdiction. Also in 1968, the International District Improvement Association (Inter*Im), a multi-ethnic group representing the entire District, was established. Formed largely by businesspersons to improve economic conditions, Inter*Im received funding from the city's Model Cities Program and sought to develop plans for community improvement.

As the District approached the 1970s, the census showed that most of the 1,600 residents in the International District were retired, elderly, single persons. Slightly more than half the District's residents were Asians; Filipinos were the largest Asian group with 400, followed by Chinese at around 375 and Japanese dwindling to about 100. Whites comprised the bulk of the balance along with about 100 African Americans. The District's population had never been so low; it had dropped some 40 percent from what it was just two decades earlier. The only people who remained in the area were poor folks who had nowhere else to go, the majority of them elderly. Some 60 percent of the "unrelated individuals" in the area lived below the poverty level, surviving on pension or social security checks. Of the small number of families in the area - most of them Chinese - 40 percent also had incomes below the poverty level.

The Honorable Wing Luke

Wing Luke was serving his first term on the Seattle City Council when, in 1965, he died in an airplane crash. In his honor, the Wing Luke Asian Museum in the International District and Wing Luke Elementary School on Beacon Hill were named after him.

Luke was a rare individual. He made history practically every time he did anything.

Besides playing a leading role in changing local conditions, particularly the rights of minorities, he established many precedents. He was the first Chinese to hold a high appointed state position, the first Chinese to run for a major political office in the state, the first Asian public office-holder in the state, and the first minority to sit on the Seattle City Council.

Earliest Immigrants

The Luke family was one of the earliest Chinese immigrant families to settle in Seattle. "My family has its roots here," he once said. "We have been here more than 80 years. My paternal grandfather operated a laundry here in the early days. Henry Yesler was one of his customers." Luke's family operated a laundry in the University District.

Wing Luke, however, was born in China. He came here at the age of five. "The first words I learned were 'yes,' 'no,' and 'he hit me first,'" Luke once told the press. "Not being able to speak English, there were lots of misunderstandings and boyhood fights," he explained.

Luke attended northend schools and quickly adapted to his new environment. Always an outstanding student, he showed signs of leadership in politics at an early age. He first ran for office at John Marshall Junior High School, where he was elected Boy's Club president. At Roosevelt High School, he was elected Boy's Club president.

Served in Military

Midway through his senior year of high school, Luke was inducted into the Army to serve in WWII. He won a bronze medal and received six combat stars during the war. Yet eventually Luke graduated with honors, earning a degree in political science and going on to American University in Washington D.C. to do graduate work in the same field. He returned to the University of Washington to obtain a law degree and entered private practice for two years before being appointed State Assistant Attorney General, serving as chief legal counsel for the Board Against Discrimination and Real Estate Division in 1957.

After five years with the Attorney General's Office, Luke decided to run for public office. At 36, he took a leave of absence from his job and filed for City Council Position 5, which had a field of nine other candidates.

A Tough City Council Race

Despite his heavy involvement with the Democratic Party since his college days, Luke knew that winning the council seat would not be easy. "The novelty of being Oriental does not help," Luke said in an interview after he won the election. "Being an Oriental does single one out, and one therefore has to work harder. The political Oriental image is not here as yet like in Hawaii, although it is getting that way."

What Luke did not expect during his campaign were slanderous smear tactics. "During the primary, fraternities at the University of Washington were asked to help door-bell [go door-to-door] for Wing," said Luke's sister Bettie. Some did. But one fraternity doorbelled against him and went out of its way to suggest that Luke was a communist, she said.

Luke won the primary and faced Dr. J.G. (Joe) Aiken, a West Seattle physician and surgeon, for the council seat. All the candidates who were eliminated in the primary gave their support to Aiken in the general election. Their endorsement, however, could not stop the growing support for Luke. In a desperate attempt to defeat Luke, another smear campaign was initiated against him. "An anonymous group printed and passed out flyers insinuating that Wing was associated with communists," recalled Bettie. "The flyer alluded to a news item in the *Peoples World* about Wing's candidacy and alleged that he was supported by communist sympathizers."

But there was no stopping Luke. Labor, educators, leaders of the major racial groups, Democrats, and Republicans endorsed him. "I had the written endorsement of prominent Seattle citizens who represented an extremely broad cross-section of the community," remarked Luke.

Luke ran a well-organized campaign with some 800 to 1,000 volunteers, mostly young people. But his biggest supporter and worker was himself. He spent some $10,000 of his own money on the election and spent many hours attending "coffee hours" and doorbelling.

Luke's campaign signs flooded the District. Chinese restaurants distributed factory-made fortune cookies that contained a message to vote for Luke.

When the election was over, Luke was an overwhelming victor. Despite the smear campaigns, Luke produced the greatest margin of victory in that year's election, some 30,000 more votes than his opponent.

On March 13, 1962, Wing Luke began his term on the Seattle City Council. "As the first person of Chinese ancestry ever to run for public office in Washington state, I have a great obligation to serve well," said Luke when he took office. "I accept that challenge of the job, in the spirit of my family, of which I am very proud."

Luke never forgot his family, with whom he kept close ties. Since grade school and as a council member, the industrious Luke worked at his family business. "When he was on the council, he would stack groceries and talk to the customers," said Bettie.

Fought for Civil Rights

As a council member Luke fought particularly hard for civil rights, urban renewal, historic preservation, and a plan to ease the downtown parking problem. A liberal member of a very conservative council, he often stood alone on issues.

Perhaps no other issue meant more to Luke than civil rights. A staunch advocate for equal opportunity for all races, Luke took the entire council on almost single-handedly concerning the issue of open housing. Shortly after he took office, at a tense, packed council meeting, he maneuvered the conservative council to commit themselves to pass an open housing ordinance. (Seattle's Open Housing Ordinance, however, was not passed until 1968.)

Despite a busy schedule, Luke served on the Board of Directors for the Urban League, Chinese Community Service Organization, and Jackson Street Community Council.

Politician and Intellectual with Promise

Emmett Watson, a reporter, pointed Luke out at the time as being "the only Seattle politician that can be described as an intellectual." Another journalist said of Luke that he "is better informed on more local, national, and international issues than almost anyone I know."

Wing Luke was a confident and ambitious person who had aspirations for higher political office. "If a man has no more ambition than to stay where he is, he'll soon burn himself out," Luke observed. "I feel I'm capable of filling any elective job in the state. I have no set design on any office, but I'm young enough to think that opportunities will manifest themselves."

Wing Luke. International Examiner file photo.

In a poll taken among Seattle voters just before his death, Luke drew the highest rating of any council person. He was "best known" by a wide margin and topped the list on all five categories- "good, active, powerful, brave, and wise." With his popularity, Luke had a bright future. He might easily have been the mayor of Seattle or Governor of Washington.

Blighted buildings. International Examiner file photo.

A major factor in the loss of residents was the inadequate supply of safe and decent housing. By the early 1970s, over half of the District's 45 hotels and apartment buildings had closed due to deterioration. Moreover, many old hotels that remained open were threatened with closure because they failed to meet the city's fire and building code requirements; codes were more stringent after the Ozark Hotel fire in downtown Seattle. The Ozark Ordinance required the installation of sprinkler systems in every commercial building and hotel, which was too expensive for many District property owners. Business conditions in the area had also stagnated by the late 1960s as the regional economy soured. The bulk of the District's 139 commercial-residential businesses provided Chinese or Japanese goods or services and depended heavily on non-resident clientele. Some storefronts were vacant, businesses were closed, and many merchants were lucky to make ends meet.

By the mid-1970s, however, the District began reviving. Ironically, the catalyst in this turnaround was the 1971 decision to construct the King County domed stadium next to the District. Residents, community groups, and their supporters worried about the stadium's impact on the District, fearing the District would become a parking lot, overrun by motels and other stadium-related businesses, and suffer traffic congestion during stadium events. Most importantly, they feared the loss of residents and the ethnic identity of the area. "Preserve the International District" became the rallying cry for supporters of the area, and in the process of fighting the stadium, a new power structure evolved in this small neighborhood.

The Kingdome Battle

In 1968, King County voters passed the $334 million Forward Thrust bond program to finance a variety of public improvement projects, including some $40 million for a multipurpose stadium to attract major league football and baseball. Three years later, after some disputes about where the stadium should be located, the stadium commission recommended a site owned by Burlington Northern Railroad, next to the King Street Railway Station and adjacent to the International District. The King County Council approved the recommendation in November 1971 and quickly appropriated funds to purchase the site. Then, in early 1972, it was announced that five hotels in the District would close because they failed to meet the new fire and building code requirements under the Ozark Ordinance. Asian American community activists associated the closures with the new stadium and charged that the closures were part of a scheme to clear land in the area for parking lots. This belief was reinforced when they learned that only 6,500 on-site parking spaces were planned for the stadium, far short of what was needed to accommodate a capacity crowd of 65,000.

At the stadium groundbreaking on November 2, 1972, a group of some 40 or so young Asian American protesters disrupted the ceremony. As King County Executive John D. Spellman, former football star Hugh McEllheny, and other political and labor leaders stood at the grandstand, protesters chanted "Stop the stadium" and hurled mud at the dignitaries. The ceremony was cut short because of the protest, although Spellman, one of several hit with mud, was able to plant a home plate in the turf. City Councilman Lem Tuai was confronted by Asian American activists, who accused him of being on the wrong side of the issue. "I believe in the stadium and think that the people in Seattle want it to be built, and I represent all the people of Seattle," Tuai told them. Many of the activists were college students, inspired by the Civil Rights Movement of the 1960s and eager to find a community cause during an era of social change. Among these were Al Kurimura, Mayumi Tsutakawa, Norris and Peter Bacho, Elaine Ikoma Ko, Shari Woo, Al and Dick Sugiyama, Frank Irigon, Sabino Cabildo, and the Domingo brothers, Silme and Nemesio. Other supporters included Larry Gossett, former leader of the Black Students Association at the University of Washington and head of the university's Educational Opportunity Program's Black Students' Division, Tyree Scott and Michael Woo of the United Construction Workers Association (UCWA), and Roberto Maestas and Juan Bocanegra of El Centro de la Raza.

The elderly rally for decent nursing. Cindy Domingo photo.

Not all community organizations took an official position on the stadium issue. Significantly, Chong Wa and the traditional Chinese associations were silent. However, the Chinatown Chamber of Commerce and CCSO voted in favor of the stadium because they thought it would stimulate business in the area. The Japanese American Citizens League (JACL), whose local office was located in the District, was also silent on the issue, as was the Japanese Hotel Association. As the Japanese population in the neighborhood had decreased, the interest of these organizations was limited. Despite the large number of Filipinos in the District, the Filipino Community, Inc., considered the voice of the Filipinos in Seattle, also did not take an official stand on the stadium.

The groups heavily involved with the stadium issue were generally district-wide and pan-Asian American. Primarily made up of Chinese, Japanese and Filipinos, they reflected the area's historical makeup and, perhaps more significantly, the emergence of

the "Asian American Movement." These groups were Inter*Im, the International District Youth Council (a group of high school and college students) and the International District Economic Association (IDEA) (a group of business owners led by Tomio Moriguchi). The International Drop-In Center, which offered cultural and social services for Filipino elderly, and the Youth Council were both firmly opposed to construction of the stadium next to the District. Donnie Chin, Mike Kozu and Greg Aramaki were leaders in the Youth Council's fight against the stadium. IDEA favored it, thinking it would bring additional customers to District restaurants and shops.

Some groups used the stadium as a vehicle to call attention to the social, economic, and physical deterioration of the neighborhood. Under the leadership of Bob Santos, who became executive director in 1972, Inter*Im was recognized by the city as the primary community-wide agency represent-

ing the area. Two residents sat on its board, along with several respected area business owners and civic-minded professionals including architect/veteran community advocate Ben Woo and Uwajimaya president Tomio Moriguchi. Equally important, Inter*Im was now the only agency whose membership represented all the ethnic groups and interests in the District. Believing the new stadium would attract customers to the District, Inter*Im nevertheless expressed concern over issues such as poor housing, deteriorated buildings, lack of social services, and a predominantly non-English-speaking elderly population living on limited incomes. Also expressed were fears that the domed stadium would displace the poor and elderly, create traffic congestion, and encourage stadium-related developments like parking lots, motels and fast-food chains. Another concern of Inter*Im's was the stagnation of businesses in the neighborhood; this concern, however, was raised even more vigorously by IDEA. Both groups, but

Donnie Chin and the International District Emergency Center

The International District is undeniably a tourist attraction. Greyhound and other tour buses grind their way through the streets during the day, occasionally stopping just enough for the tourist to take pictures of Hing Hay Park or to eat at one of the restaurants in the area.

Yet at night, flashing neon signs invite passersby into some of the same restaurants and bars. Meanwhile, down the alley, a drunk is rolled. Across the street in one of the old hotels, an old man having an heart attack is gasping for air. Soon, before Medic One gets there, a guy dressed in uniform with a first aid kit runs towards the hotel, stopping momentarily at the alley to see if the drunk is okay.

Donnie Chin. International Examiner file phto.

For over three decades, Donnie Chin has been a watchdog providing emergency medical services to those in the District. Well-trained in providing such services, he has won the respect of the fire department and Medic One, ambulance services, health centers, and the police.

Since 1968, when Chin was in junior high school, long before there were health clinic or social service agencies in the area, Chin realized that the police and fire department (among others) were slow to respond to District emergencies, if at all. Calling themselves Asians for Unity Emergency Squad, Chin and his friend Dean Wong started buying medical equipment and researching emergency aid programs and services.

A little later, they took up the name International District Emergency Center and began patrolling the streets, responding to medical, emotional, and personal traumas —usually before Medic One or the police reached the scene. These have included fires, shootings, assaults, car accidents, and even cut fingers. They have also responded to non-emergencies such as water leaks, blackouts, broken windows, and personal safety matters which are less pressing but nonetheless of vital concern to area residents.

While developing the Emergency Center in the early 1970s, Chin was also a leader in the now-defunct International District Youth Council fighting the Kingdome. One program that operated out of the Youth Council was the first food bank program in the District. Started by Norris Bacho, Chin operated the food pro-gram along with Annie Galarosa.

For over three decades, Chin has been a pillar in the District. Although he has garnered much praise for the hundreds of lives he has saved, and for his dedication and services, he is nevertheless an unsung hero of sorts.

Having to deal with verbal abuse from the drug pushers and junkies, prostitutes, gang members and gangsters, thugs, criminals and other deviants in the District for years —just to help those in need —is no easy chore. Still, Chin has been doing it all for over 30 years.

Absolutely no one has saved more lives or helped make the District a safer place to live than Donnie Chin, a paramount figure in the area and community.

particularly IDEA, pressured the city to promote development of commerce in the area by preserving ethnic businesses and attracting diverse new private investments.

The city's response to this gamut of concerns was to release some of its staff to work with the community. The Department of Human Resources assigned three staff persons to Inter*Im to assess housing conditions in the area. Meanwhile, concerned citizens and merchants in Pioneer Square began to ask what impact the stadium might have on their neighborhood. This led to the formation of the Citizens Action Force, a committee jointly appointed by the Mayor and County Executive to study and make recommendations to minimize the stadium's impact on surrounding areas. The committee included representatives from Pioneer Square and three persons from the International District: Sue Molman, acting director of Inter*Im; Wesley Tao, who operated an insurance agency; and Carlos Young, owner of an engineering firm in the area.

Planting the Seeds of a New Infrastructure

Three months later, the Citizens Action Force, working with the city's Department of Community Development (DCD), presented its recommendations to the City Council. Most of their recommendations were incorporated into the city's "South Central Business District Policies For Action," a set of resolutions passed by the City Council in September 1972. The document contained 21 policies and action items to minimize the stadium's adverse impacts and to preserve the International District and Pioneer Square neighborhoods. It included a promise to conduct a feasibility study on developing an Asian cultural center in the

International District, several plans to help revitalize the area, and an effort to seek federal funds to develop housing in the District. The county contracted Diana Bower, who had worked with the Seattle Model Cities Program, to work with the Citizens Action Force and to coordinate stadium mitigation efforts.

One of the Council's resolutions was to make the International District a "special review district" with overlay (additional) zoning regulations, over existing zoning, to control land use in the area; thus, the International Special Review District Board was established in August 1973. Initially conceived to mitigate the stadium's impact, the Review Board's purpose expanded to "preserve the District's unique Asian character and to encourage the rehabilitation of areas for housing and new pedestrian-oriented business." Planner Glenn Chinn, one of the first Review Board members, and city staffperson Don Erickson were instrumental in setting up the board. The Special Review Board was given broad power to recommend development guidelines and zoning regulations, which could modify the regular zoning laws, and to approve or disapprove of proposed structural changes. Although City officials have the final say, the City has seldom (if ever) overturned a Review Board recommendation.

In its early days the Special Review Board largely catered to District businesses, amending its rules to accommodate business several times. When confronted with organized groups of residents, the Board also yielded to their demands. On one occasion, the Review Board decided to reserve all street-level space for "pedestrian-oriented" - meaning retail - businesses. This meant all community service organizations, associations and

social clubs would have to relocate above ground level. Upon learning of the proposed regulation, the Chong Wa Benevolent Association asked for a public hearing. About a hundred Chinese showed up in angry protest, arguing that Chinese associations were important gathering places for the elderly men in Chinatown and had long been located in street-level storefronts. Also in protest, the Chinese withdrew their savings - rumored to be one million dollars - from the neighborhood Seafirst Bank (now Bank of America), where the Review Board chairperson was branch manager. The chairperson soon resigned from the Board, as did a Chinese American architect who was ridiculed by community members, and the regulation was modified to permit associations and other "non-pedestrian" uses to remain at street level.

Another Board incident involved a developer who wanted to build a low-income housing project within the King Street Core. The project, approved by the Department of Housing and Urban Development (HUD) for low-interest financing, violated the development guidelines established by the Special Review Board. The Board requested HUD's approval for another proposed project in the District that met all the regulations, and a public hearing to hear what the community had to say. About 75 persons, mostly elderly Chinese residents who were members of the International District Housing Alliance, came to support the King Street Core project. Those who spoke told the Board of the poor housing conditions in the area; a local merchant told Board members that many elderly Chinese residents came to his store to sign up for new housing. Days later, the Board amended its regulations to allow the developer to build, despite the objections of some merchants on the Board. Said one merchant, "Low-income people don't have money. We want the space for something else." Eventually, the Board and others in the District got the city to persuade HUD's regional office to approve both projects.

Also in the 1970s, the Seattle Chinatown-International District Preservation and Development Authority (SCIDPDA), a public corporation, was established to develop, own, and manage property for the community's benefit. Inter*Im board members had discussed developing a public corporation as early as 1973, when the Pike Place Market was the only Seattle neighborhood with such an entity. Earlier that year, the Seattle City Council had approved $200,000 as "seed money" to develop an Asian cultural center in the District. After some discussion, the community agreed the money should be used to develop a community center to house social service agencies and provide space for cultural activities. Eventually, Inter*Im persuaded the City Council to allocate additional funds ($185,000) for the center in the fall of 1974. However, under state law the city could not legally give the money to the District. The city then suggested forming a public corporation -with the power to receive public funds - in order to develop and own the community center. Led by Barry Mar , Inter*Im worked with a law firm and the city's legal office to finish a draft of the new corporation's charter in late 1974.

The draft appeared to meet with the approval of all District groups - including many Chinese - except Chong Wa. Chong Wa insisted that the draft be translated into Chinese, argued that the wording was too difficult for laymen to understand, and demanded that no action be taken until after

Chinese New Year, in March 1975. Another meeting was scheduled for January 1975, when the material would be translated and distributed for discussion. In early January, however, Chong Wa sent a letter to Inter*Im and the Mayor's office announcing that it could not approve or support the development of the corporation. Nevertheless, members of Chong Wa appeared at the January meeting complaining again of the difficulty of the language in the charter, and that the corporation had "too much power."

A committee which included Chong Wa members was established to review and modify the draft where necessary. Within two months, the committee had completed its task and circulated the document, including a Chinese version, for discussion. With no opposition, Inter*Im submitted the draft to the Mayor's Office for approval with 120 signatures, including the names of Chong Wa members who had inadvertently signed. Meanwhile, in a complete reversal, Chong Wa submitted its own application for a public corporation, with nearly the same language as the one submitted by Inter*Im. However, Chong Wa's application was to establish a "Chinatown" rather than an "International District" Preservation and Development Authority, with boundaries limited to the King

City Councilperson Dolores Sibonga was instrumental in getting city funds for the District. International Examiner file photo.

Street Core, where most of the Chinese businesses were.

Faced with two competing applications, Mayor Ulhman compromised by establishing the "Seattle Chinatown/International District Public Development Authority" (SCIDPDA) in late September, after successfully withstanding a recall election to remove him from office. The mayor's representative and International District manager, James Mason, had already announced that there would be no "radicals" on the new

Committee for the Corrective Action Program

Frustrated by the lack of action by King County, city government and federal agencies to the concerns and problems facing the International District, a group of young activist established the Committee for the Corrective Action Program in late 1974. Many of those were involved with the group had just graduated from or still in college. They included those who were, politically, from the far left to those in the middle. The purpose of the committee was to established a "united front" among a broad range of Asian community groups that would pressure and lobby King County government over a list of demands.

Among the active leaders with the Committee where Silme Domingo, Neil Asaba, Michael Woo, Steve Lock, Kenny Mar, Nemesio Domingo, Kyle Kinoshita, Elaine Ko, Edmon Lee, Paul Ong, Jackie Lum, Frank Irigon, and Shari Woo.

On December 28, 1974, representatives from a various groups and individuals presented a number of proposals at a meeting on what the County should do to improve the conditions in the District, and to minimize the impacts of the stadium on the area. From that meeting, eight demands, which were sent to King County Executive John Spellman, emerged:

1. Award the service and concession contracts to a designated non-profit organization to deal with the adverse impacts of the stadium and other related problems with the District and the surrounding Asian American community;
2. Rewrite stadium specifications requiring

Larry Gossett speaking to demonstrators at the occupation of King County Executive John Spellman's office. International Examiner file photo.

40 apprenticeship and 40 journeymen positions for Asian Americans;
3. Build and furnish 1000 low-income housing units in the District;
4. Establish a "user's tax" on all stadium activities which will be used to fund community projects to minimize stadium impacts;
5. Establish a multi-service center for senior citizens in the District;
6. Establish and maintain a health clinic in the District;
7. Free admission to all stadium events for elderly residents of the District; and
8. Retain a full-time consultant for the stadium's impact.

When efforts to meet with Spellman over the demands did not materialize, the Committee called for a public demonstration. On February 3, some 200 demonstrators convened at Hing Hay Park in the District to listen to a couple of speakers denounce Spellman and county officials. From there, they proceeded to the County Courthouse, where they march four floors to Spellman's office demanding to speak with him. When told that the county executive was not there, the protesters proceeded to go directly to Spellman's office to look for him. Spellman was no where to be found and so the demonstrators just took over his office.

A short time later, Spellman did meet with members from the Committee for the Corrective Action Program and agreed to pursue funding for a health clinic in the District and to encourage the general contractor for the stadium to hire Asian Americans.

corporation's board. The mayor then appointed a board of twelve members. Four appointees came from a list of nominees submitted by Inter*Im (which apparently had "radicals" among them), four from a list submitted by Chong Wa, and four were appointed by the Mayor's Office. In a letter to both Inter*Im and Chong Wa, Mayor Ulhman stated his intention to appoint persons who could "work with private business and the financial community to attract private capital to complement and augment public monies."

The new PDA bought the Bush Hotel in 1978 and began renovating the building. It was the first building in the District to be renovated in years. Renamed the Bush-Asia Center, it now provides retail space, low-income housing, transient housing, and office space for social service agencies, along with a meal program for the District's elderly residents and space for community events. In addition, the PDA also purchased an old garage on Seventh Avenue, off Jackson Street, and converted it into a theater for the Northwest Asian American Theatre group and a facility for the Wing Luke Asian Museum, which moved from its original facility on Eighth Avenue. The PDA also acquired the old New Central Hotel from the Nishimura family in the early 1980s. The upper floors of the New Central were renovated for several purposes: 28 units of housing for the elderly; retail/office space for the ground floor and lower floors; and the Denise Louie Child Care Center, which had to move from the old Bailey Gatzert School due to demolition.

It was Shigeko Uno who arranged the PDA's acquisition of the Bush Hotel. She was the property manager for Rainier Heat and Power, which owned the hotel as well as several other buildings in the District. Several years earlier, she had persuaded Tomio Moriguchi to acquire and construct a new Uwajimaya supermarket on a block owned by Rainier Heat and Power. Uno, whose parents owned the White River Dairy at Eighth and Weller prior to World War II, had grown up in the District. In 1947, she became the

Ben Woo headed the Public Development Authority and was a leader in the International District. International Examiner file photo.

first woman president of the Seattle chapter of the Japanese American Citizens League. An active civic participant for years, Uno later became a SCIDPDA board member and in the early 1980s oversaw the sale of several Rainier Heat and Power properties.

Community Grows in Kingdome's Shadow

Although the Kingdome was built next to the District, activists had succeeded in drawing attention to the neighborhood's pressing needs. Government at all levels (city, county, state and federal) had responded to the activists' demands by providing regulatory, financial and programmatic assistance to preserve and revitalize the historic neighborhood as well as to help its low-income residents. Moreover, a well-organized and politically astute community network had by now formed, to help the District gain recognition and access to local government resources and funding.

By the close of the 1970s, three high-rises for the elderly were built in the District: Imperial House, International House, and International Terrace, a high-rise constructed by the Seattle Housing Authority. They became part of a safety net for the elderly that included a free food program operated by the Youth Council and a free lunch program. Meanwhile, the county and city funded the International District Health Clinic, a new health-care facility. Inter*Im created the International District Housing Alliance and the Denise Louie Child Care Center. The center was named after a young District activist, accidentally killed by shotgun fire during a gang dispute while eating at a San Francisco Chinatown restaurant. Asian Counseling and Referral Service, now a multi-program agency serving Asian Americans and others throughout the county, also began in the late 1970s and was initially housed at Inter*Im offices on Jackson Street. A group of Chinese, mostly students from the University of Washington, started Chinese Information and Service Center (CISC), orienting their services to-

The Milwaukee Hotel Occupation
by Melissa Lin

In 1977, a group of housing activists, inspired by the occupation of the International Hotel in San Francisco's Chinatown, took over the Milwaukee Hotel. One of the International District's larger, older and more dilapidated hotels, the Milwaukee was a prime candidate for closure under the Ozark Ordinance. City inspectors had found some 60 code violations and the hotel's owners were ready to close. To stop the closure and the eviction of tenants, the activists agreed to help the owners fix the code violations, which they did in a mere three weeks.

They then occupied the hotel and kept it open for a year and a half. Volunteers maintained a 24-hour fire watch inside the building, relocated residents, cleaned out the building, secured doors, built fire doors, and started repairs. Over 300 volunteers participated over a period of three years. Joe Kitamura, a long-time District resident, served as volunteer janitor for the building. Perry Lee, an employee at the King County Health Department, got the city to help by hauling out over twenty tons of garbage. Andy Mizuki, one of the firewatch volunteers, remembers writing out instructions on the doors, telling how to get in and out of the building through the newly secured fire doors. "My handwriting is still on every door in that building."

The Milwaukee also benefited from hundreds of hours of volunteer labor donated by various segments of the community. Mizuki relates, "Tyree Scott did the electrical work for free, people from El Centro and Bernie Whitebear's people, old and young people all contributed their time." The volunteers installed the new fire alarm system because they didn't have the money to pay a professional. However, says Mizuki, a Latino-owned company designed the system, bought materials, secured the permits and instructed the volunteers in how to install the system. "We installed it in 2 or 3 weeks; they had said it would take two or three months," Mizuki recalls.

Other volunteers at the time included Elaine Ko, Tommy Mar, Richard Mar, Suzy Chin, Donnie Chin, and Bob Santos. The volunteers held potlucks to raise money, and work parties to fix up the hotel's rooms. "We would hold a work party one day and fix up one room, and another work party another day on another room, and so on. The Milwaukee really brought the community together."

Meanwhile, the volunteers had also managed to raise enough money to buy the building. However, their offer was refused, and the three-year occupation ended with an orderly retreat. The volunteers helped relocate the residents to other buildings

Milwaukee hotel. International Examiner file photo.

nearby.

In spite of the setback, the Milwaukee occupation was a turning point for the movement to preserve affordable housing in the District because it accentuated and sustained the pressure on public officials to provide assistance to improve housing conditions in the area. Today, many of the original Milwaukee activists are still involved in the issue of affordable housing, while a whole new generation, inspired by the Milwaukee, has entered the arena. To this day, says Santos, "Folks nationwide look at the International District as an example of what one neighborhood can accomplish."

A History of Asian Community Media (excerpted)

(Mayumi Tsutakawa, *International Examiner*, June 15, 1983)

The *International Examiner*, like many other alternative and homespun community media...ha[s] thanklessly persisted....Gone are the *Filipino Forum, Bayanihan Tribune* and *Northwest Indian News*. New are *Seattle Chinese Post* and *King Street Mediaworks*...still chugging along with us are the *Asian Family Affair, Filipino Herald,* and *North American Post*.

Community media has been with us since the early immigrants arrived at these golden shores. The foreign language press quickly followed the path of immigration settlement. Not only the Swedish, Russian and German communities, but virtually every ethnic group had its press....The early Afro-American communities also had what whites termed "the race press," offering literature and news written by Black America's greatest writers.

The ethnic press usually printed practical information for immigrants. But sentimental vignettes, community social and sports news, as well as news of the old country always made their way onto its pages.

At the turn of the century, the Japanese community in the Northwest supported, at times, five Japanese language dailies. In fact, all the Asian American communities here featured active presses, reflecting the high level of literacy among immigrants. In the early Japanese community...[l]eftist political diatribes, literary journals and women's/home magazines were written and printed with fervor.

James Sakamoto's *Japanese American Courier*, the first English language paper published in the Northwest, helped to develop the fledgling Japanese American Citizens League and aided in the Americanization process for the second generation Nisei....

The *North American Post*, our surviving Japanese language newspaper, began after the war's end as a weekly and later became a daily. The current editor, Takami Hibiya, has been with it under several publishers, having joined the staff in 1956. Now published three times a week, the paper is making the transition from hand-picked type and letter press printing...to photographically typeset and offset print methods. H.T. Kubota is now the publisher.

....In the 70s at least three Filipino newspapers vied for attention in Seattle. Martin and Dolores Sibonga published the *Filipino Forum* from 1977 to 1978. A monthly paper, it urged others to take part in "united minority action" and the often militant, civil rights movement of the time.

The *Bayanihan Tribune*, edited by Dione Corsilles from about 1974 to 1979, was a bi-weekly newspaper which many of the young activists of the early Asian American movement called the most progressive newspaper. It offered opinions often running counter to the Marcos regime which was beginning to strangle civil rights in the Philippines. [The] publisher was Ely U. Orias.

Emiliano "Frank" Francisco's *Filipino American Herald* has been the longest lasting of these newspapers and has been published monthly since 1968. His has been called the most conservative Filipino newspaper, often featuring pro-American and pro-Philippine government news prominently in the newspaper, although the publication had its roots in the early Cannery Workers Union, founded in 1934.

In 1970, in the early days of the Asian American movement, Nemesio Domingo and Sabino Cabildo published *Kapisanan*. After about a year, the newspaper was changed to *Asian Family Affair* (AFA)....The founders of AFA were Diane Wong, Norman Mar, Al Sugiyama and Frankie Irigon[.]

...[T]he *International Examiner* was founded in 1974 to publish monthly news of the International District. Since then, under editor Ron Chew's [direction], the newspaper has become a biweekly, and covers wider issues of importance to Asian Americans in the entire region.

Dat Moi (New Land) *Newspaper*, in the Vietnamese language, has been published since 1975. A biweekly publication, now under the leadership of Giang Van Nguyen, it is sold for $1.25 a copy and sponsored by a nonprofit corporation[.]

The *Kingstreet Mediaworks*...has provided training and backup media work for many community agencies. Begun in 1978 by Dean Wong, John Harada, Jeff Hanada and Mark Mano, the group has provided workshops in photography and video....

The Seattle Chinese Post, a Chinese language weekly, is the first in that language since before the war. (The English version of the Post was changed to the *Northwest Asian Weekly*.) Prior to the *Post*'s founding by publisher Assunta Ng [in 1981], the Chinese community was served by radio programs, principally on *KRAB-FM*. The Chinese programs, produced by two different groups, are still presented on alternate weeks. Vietnamese and Filipino programs, however...have been cut off the air of that community access station. There seems to have been a lack of support and perhaps understanding of the programs by the station's board and staff.

Why does the community press continue to play an important role while community members, individually and collectively, are making steady and sure inroads to representation, jobs and political clout I established government, education and business circles? I think four factors can be pointed out:

- Self-determination - We can make it on our own.
- Truth and Accuracy - We know best what happens and how it happens in our community.
- Realistic Outlook - We present a picture of ourselves that is neither all crime and violence, nor all sugar-coated kimono-clad dolls.
- Communication Network - Community cohesion and a sense of pride is boosted by the community media.

It is unfortunate that the majority of community members seem to take advantage of the community media by using them, but not actively supporting them. Too many Asians, like the general population, have been lured into the mindset that the major media have the market on glamour and excitement. Just seeing the ripple of excitement that passes through a community meeting when television cameras are present or an Asian television news person agrees to participate in some community event is an example of this unfortunate thinking.

The community media representatives need to be included when sending out press releases, announcing press conferences and handing out complimentary tickets; and their presence should be thankfully acknowledged, for the community media people are the most hardworking and loyal supporters of the community.

Moreover, the community needs to see its community media workers as professional journalists, as people who need to work for a living and not just volunteering their time for the community. We don't ask dentists to work for free, yet this often happens with photographers, designers and writers in the community.

At the same time, journalists need to [subscribe] to the accepted canons of journalism as much as anyone. Accuracy is paramount. Timeliness is nice, as is interesting presentation of the news. But fairness and ethical reporting are two factors by which we are ultimately judged. We need to write stories about more than just our friends, and business associates. It's usually faster and easier to write about someone we know, but does it serve the reader? We don't need to be completely unbiased to the point that there is no advocacy, after all. *We are the alternative to the establishment media.* However, if in the course of covering a community issue we find that there is more than one point of view within the community, don't we have the responsibility and obligation to seek out representatives of all sides of the agreement?

For that matter, single-source stories (only interviewing one person on a particular topic) are never as interesting or compelling to a reader as multi-source stories. Sure, the interview with a single, fascinating individual is something you can't pass up, but when a general topic such as dance or social services or business crops up, it's worth it to the reader to see more than "expert's" opinion.

In my opinion, Asian community newspapers have always had the corner on high-quality design and production. Perhaps the Asian graphic, and technical penchant shows up here. But these characteristics should never take the place of dynamic and well-edited writing on the week's important subjects.

In the editorial department, I notice some Asian community papers are hesitant to take advantage of the editor's privilege of spouting off on various topics in editorials. But.... [C]ommunity media have [often] served as effective training grounds for those who have found good positions in the major radio and television and newspapers in this region or have formed successful graphic arts businesses. Some have gone on to legal or political work. Mark Mano is in production at KING-TV, Terri Nakamura and Victor Kubo are successful graphic artists, Dione Corsilles has a printing company and, of course, Dolores Sibonga is a City Councilmember.

wards recent Chinese immigrants and the Chinese elderly. After operating on a volunteer basis for a couple of years out of the old Wing Luke Museum on Eighth Avenue, CISC finally got funding from King County United Way.

The State's Department of Social and Health Services, for its part, established a multi-Asian-language project to locate and enroll eligible residents in the District for its financial and elderly services programs. Operating out of the Morrison Hotel, where the department's Pioneer Square office was located, caseworkers fluent in Cantonese, Japanese and Tagalog went from hotel to hotel to find eligible residents. It was the first Asian-language unit ever established by a state agency. The Department of Social and Health Services' Health Division (now a separate state department) also provided funds to support the operations of the International District Health Clinic beginning in the early 1980s.

With very few public open spaces, the District made the best of what it had. Hing Hay Park, at the center of the District, was designed by Don Sakuma and constructed in 1975. The Republic of China and the Taiwan government provided the Chinese pavilion in the park. On the hillside next to the freeway, Kobe Terrace Park was constructed at the end of the decade, with Japanese exhibits provided by Seattle's sister city, Kobe, Japan. A mini-park for District children was suggested by lifelong resident and IDEC leader Donnie Chin and presented to the city for funding by Diana Bower. Although the city allocated funds in 1975, the Seattle Parks Department took five years to find an adequate site and to construct the mini-park at Seventh Avenue and Lane Street. Designed by Joey Ing's architectural firm and one of the earliest city-funded

projects, the park included Gerard Tsutakawa's sculptured dragon within a sandy play area, a covered pavilion, and a bamboo jungle.

Inter*Im and others proposed building a pea-patch garden in the District, but did not receive funding from the city or county. Nevertheless, Inter*Im was able to convince Danny Woo to allow the development of a community garden where the elderly could grow vegetables. The Woo family owned a parcel of undeveloped land on a steep hillside on the north side of Main Street, next to the International Terrace Apartments. With minimal funding, volunteer labor, and donated material and equipment, Inter*Im, along with Darlyn Rundberg, developed the Danny Woo Community Garden. Terraces were cut into the hillside by Ohno Landscape Company and railroad ties and utility poles were used to construct retaining walls. Horse manure from Longacres racing track was used to rotovate with existing clay and 300 cubic yards of sand. University of Washington architecture students designed and helped construct the garden. The Danny Woo property is leased to Inter*Im, which manages the garden, while the city right-of-way portion of the garden was turned over to Inter*Im for community use. An annual pig roast has been held at the garden every summer since 1975.

The creation of the Special Review District proved to be an effective mechanism in preserving the neighborhood's character; it prevented stadium-related facilities such as certain types of parking lots, hotels and fast food places from developing in the area. To the disappointment of many in the business sector, however, stadium traffic added very little to the patronage of District restaurants and shops. In fact, vehicular traffic brought the District to gridlock on game days, tak-

ing up all on and off-street parking, and even curtailing access to the area. Many businesses, particularly restaurants, actually lost business on days when the stadium was filled to capacity - some 65,000 for football and 56,000 for baseball.

The Ruby Chow Factor

Ruby Chow had been a force in the Chinese community since the early 1950s. She and her husband, Ping Chow, started a Chinese restaurant on First Hill in 1947 with the help of a police officer. Chow established connections with the many politicians, busi-

Ruby Chow. Examiner file photo.

ness leaders, and journalists who dined at Ruby Chow's Restaurant, a former Italian restaurant converted from a house at 12th

Avenue and Jefferson. Through these connections, she became the leading spokesperson for the local Chinese community to the outside world for at least a half a century and a strong advocate who did much for the Chinese community, especially its youth. Some of her critics say she was too insular (directed primarily for the Chinese) and antagonistic toward other Asian American groups. Others say that she spent her energy on conflicts internal to the community rather than educating external forces - like City Hall, county government and the downtown establishment - about the community's issues. Nevertheless, Chow was a maverick who sought to bring contemporary ideas to the forefront of the Chinese community and Chinatown, and challenged head-on the traditional leadership and ideas of the Chong Wa.

In 1951, Chow was instrumental in starting the Seattle Chinese Girls' Drill Team, which has since won international acclaim and is a perennial favorite in the city's Seafair parade. In 1957, Chow, Ruth Chinn and other women became board members of the Chong Wa Benevolent Association. It was the first time in the nation that women sat with men as board members of an overseas Chinese umbrella association such as Chong Wa. "We started reforms in Chong Wa," said Chinn (the wife of Robert Chinn, who founded United Savings and Loan). "We started to have parades and queen contests under Chong Wa. We got recreation equipment for the Chinese school. I set up Chinese conversation class for the young children who haven't got the time to come every day to Chinese school. I taught citizenship and English to get many people to pass that citizenship test (1)." In the early 1960s, when the national civil rights movement reached Seattle, Ruby Chow and others started the Chinese Community Service Organization. In 1973, she ran successfully for

a seat on the King County Council and eventually served three 4-year terms representing Southeast Seattle, including the International District and unincorporated areas south of the city to Renton. At the peak of the battle over the Kingdome, she sponsored the ordinance that provided initial funds to establish the International District Health Center. Meanwhile, in 1975, Chow quietly became the first woman to achieve the presidency of a Chong Wa (an overseas Chinese association), locally and worldwide.

Six years later, her clash with Chong Wa's traditional elements erupted in the open. Upset over Chow's presidency, most of the traditional family associations and tongs withdrew from Chong Wa and formed the Alliance of Chinese Associations. With a banner reading "This Time Chinese are not for Chinese" in English and Chinese, the Alliance held a press conference prior to the 1981 primary elections to announce its support for Ron Sims, one of two candidates running against Chow for a county seat. At the news conference held in the District, Sims sat between Don Chin and Peter Wong, a District storeowner and president of the Alliance. "By tradition, Chinese are very loyal to their people," said Chin, a veteran promoter and area store owner, founder of the Chinatown Chamber of Commerce, and former Executive Director of Inter*Im. "But in the last 7 years since Chow has been in office, she has done little for the International District and, in fact, little for the entire Fifth District," Chin charged. "She's [Chow] uncooperative and inaccessible."[2] The Alliance of Chinese Associations, Chin claimed, consisted of 12 Chinese family associations and four fraternal associations, representing "75 to 80 percent of the Chinese community." Chow suggested that the Alliance opposed her because of her gender and her perceived dominance in Chong Wa, which she claimed

was "silly." In the end, Chow won the election and retained the presidency of Chong Wa. Though no longer an umbrella organization for the local Chinese community, Chong Wa has persisted in its claims to speak for the Chinese. Efforts to mend fences within the Chinese community by replacing Chow with more moderate and less political personalities, such as Ted Pang, have not succeeded.

In 1984, a group called the Chinese Community Coalition Committee was formed to help unify the splintered community; it consisted of representatives from several Chinese organizations. "We invited seven existing organizations to sit and talk among themselves and examine the possibility of merging, to form a new force that has a lot of clout, leadership, forward-looking people in the things the Chinese community really needs," said Ben Woo, the committee's president.[3] The committee grew to eight representatives and included the Chinatown/Chinese Chamber of Commerce, Chinese Community Service Organization, Chinese Community Public Affairs Organization, Chinese Parents Service Organization, Jade Guild, Seattle Chinese Athletic Association, Seattle Chinese Women's Club, and the Society of Chinese Engineers of Seattle. "The groups are not Chinatown centered, not aligned with family associations or Chinese businesses. Many are professional people in the majority society," said Woo. "All the organizations have been for themselves," added Ruth Chinn, another committee member. "The Chong Wa leaders have been for themselves. But this way, with the coalition, we are all under one umbrella." The coalition decided to work together to start a nursing home for seniors, which eventually resulted in the establishment of Kin On Nursing Home.

Domingo and Viernes Assassinated

The International District community, the Philippine independence movement, and the struggle for workers' rights were hit hard on June 1, 1981. Silme Domingo and Gene Viernes were gunned down inside the office of Local 37 of the International Longshoremen's and Warehouseman's Union at Second Avenue South and South Main Street. Viernes and Domingo were in the forefront of a movement to reform the corrupt and backward system of dispatching workers in Alaska's canneries. Both were also active in the opposition to the Marcos regime in the Philippines.

Silme Domingo was 29 years old and the secretary-treasurer of Local 37. A seasoned activist who grew up in Seattle, he and his older brother, Nemesio, had helped organize the Alaska Cannery Workers Association and the Northwest Labor Employment and Law Office (LELO), which filed racial discrimination law suits against three Alaska canneries. Both Domingo brothers had worked in the canneries. While a student at the University of Washington (UW), Silme was active with the Asian Students Coalition, Fili-pino Students Association, and Asian Family Affair newspaper. He later attended the School of Public Affairs, and was also a teaching assistant with the UW Asian American Studies Program and an intern with the Washington State Commission on Asian American Affairs. Domingo was active in the fight against the Kingdome and on the board of the International Drop-In Center, a program for elderly Filipinos. A tireless activist and father of two baby girls, Domingo was also active with the United Construction Workers Association, which fought for construction trade jobs for people

(Left to Right) Silme Domingo, Caro Eugenino, and Gene Viernes outside of Union Hall. Cannery workers' photo.

of color. Most importantly, he was a leader with the Union of Democratic Filipinos (also known as KDP), an anti-Marcos organization.

Gene Viernes was the dispatcher for the cannery union and also 29 years old at the time of his death. Originally from Wapato, Viernes worked in the canneries; he had led a food strike at Wards Cove Cannery in 1973 in a successful attempt to get fruit and fresh vegetables for the Filipino crew. He was a former director of the Alaska Cannery Workers Association, which he helped start with the Domingo brothers after the 1973 cannery season. Viernes also helped found LELO and was a plaintiff in the cannery lawsuits. Smart and knowledgeable, Viernes wrote a series of articles on the history of cannery worker exploitation and the Filipino labor leaders for the International Examiner. He also was a member of the Union of Democratic Filipinos and had visited the Philippines.

Before he died, Domingo was able to identify Jimmy Bulosan Ramil and Pompeyo Benito Guloy, Jr. as the assailants and gave their names to a fireman who jotted them on a piece of scrap paper. King County prosecuting attorney Joanne Maida would say that it was upon Domingo's strength and integrity that the case against Ramil and Guloy was won. Both Ramil and Guloy were hitmen and members of the Tulisan gang, acting on the orders of Tulisan leader Fortunado "Tony" Dictado. Viernes had refused to dispatch Tulisan members to Alaska, which hampered their ability to engage in and control gambling at the canneries and in the District. Ramil and Benito were convicted of the murders in September 1981, and sentenced to life in prison without the possibility of parole. In May 1982, Dictado was found guilty of two counts of aggravated first-degree murder.

Yet the motives for the killings ran much deeper than gambling profits. The Committee for Justice for Domingo and Viernes emerged immediately after the killings to help prosecute all those involved in the murders. The young committee leaders included Elaine Ikoma Ko; Cindy Domingo, Domingo's sister; Terri Mast, his wife; and David Della. A key target of the Committee was Constantine "Tony" Baruso, president of Local 37 at the time of the killings. Police discovered that Baruso was the registered owner of the murder weapon, a gun. He was arrested - but not charged - in July of 1981, and claimed that the gun was stolen from him. When called to testify at the trials of the three defendants, Baruso invoked the Fifth Amendment each time. Six months after the killings, in December, Baruso was ousted from the union in a recall election (along with long-time Local 37 member Abe Cruz) for vote-tampering in an international union election. Baruso was a member of the union's old guard and at odds with the reformist group led by Domingo and Viernes. Nemesio Domingo Sr., Silme's father, who was the union's Business Agent, then assumed the presidency of Local 37.

Convinced of Baruso's - and the Marcos regime's - involvement with the killing, the Committee for Justice continued to gather evidence and press for prosecution. The Committee charged that Domingo and Viernes were targets of the "Philippine Infiltration Plan," an attempt by Marcos government agents to neutralize opposition, and that Baruso participated in that scheme by providing information on members of the anti-Marcos op-

position. Eventually, with the Committee's help, prosecutors were able to gather enough evidence on Baruso to convict him of the murders and sentence him to life in prison without the possibility of parole. Finally, after a decade of evidence gathering, organizing, court hearings, and lawsuits, the Committee for Justice for Domingo and Viernes accomplished its ultimate mission in 1991. The families of Domingo and Viernes were awarded $15 million from the estate of Ferdinand Marcos for their deaths, the first time that a foreign government allied with the U.S. government was held accountable to U.S. citizens for assassinations on U.S. soil.

The Wah Mee Killings

From the beginning, the International District had a notorious reputation as a place for gambling and other vices. But what happened on February 19, 1983, was utterly shocking, despicable, and inconceivable - even for those familiar with the area's gambling, vice, and crime. Just after midnight on

International Examiner file photo.

Willie Mak. International Examiner file photo.

that Saturday evening, three young Chinese gunmen robbed, tied, and shot 14 persons, killing 13, at the Wah Mee Club on Maynard Alley just off of King Street. One was shot in the Club's office area and the others around five gambling tables. It was the single worst mass slaying incident in Seattle and the state, and one of the worst mass single-day slayings in the nation's history.

The Wah Mee Club was a private club that had recently been remodeled for security; it reopened when four business partners each agreed to put up $15,000 for high-stakes gambling. The dead victims were middle-aged and elderly, 12 men and one woman. Four were residents of the District and most were connected to the restaurant business as cooks, workers or owners. The lone survivor was Wai Chin, a 61-year-old former cook and dealer at the Club. He was tied up and shot in the jaw and neck but miraculously freed himself and managed to get outside to the alley where a passerby found him.

Chin was able to identify two of the three killers, Kwan Fai "Willie" Mak, then 22 years old, and Benjamin Kin Ng, 20. Police quickly arrested and charged both with 13 counts of aggravated first-degree murder and one count of first-degree assault. A third accomplice, Wai Chiu "Tony" Ng (no relation to Benjamin), was arrested in Canada some months later and charged with the same crimes. The motive for the killings was robbery, although the defense and some others suggested revenge or tong rivalry. All were tried and found guilty. Mak, who masterminded the crimes, was initially given the death penalty. Benjamin Ng did not receive the death penalty, to the anger and frustration of the victims' relatives (and most of the Chinese community), but received life in prison without the possibility of parole. Tony Ng was acquitted of murder charges but convicted of 13 counts of robbery and one count of assault. The jury believed he took part in the crime because Mak had threatened to kill him and his family if he did not participate.

All but one of the victims was a member of the Bing Kung Tong. Because Benjamin Ng and Willie Mak were members of the Hop Sing Tong, a rival tong, rumors quickly developed that there was more to the shooting than robbery. However, Major Dale Douglass, head of the Police Department's Criminal Investigation Division, asserted that police had thoroughly explored evidence of organized involvement by the tongs and found none. Indeed, Douglass expressed elation at the rumors of tong rivalry because it caused Hop Sing members to come forward to cooperate with the police investigation. After the conviction of Benjamin Ng, Senior Prosecutor Robert Lasnik noted that, contrary to the stereotype, "we didn't run up against the so-called traditional silence of Chinatown." Witnesses were cooperative, he added, including the younger Chinese, who stuck to their stories.

The Wah Mee killings had a profound impact on the District's image and businesses. For months, Chinese associations, the International District community, Mayor Charlie Royer, and Police Chief Patrick Fitzsimmons did everything they could to make the District appear a safe place to visit, eat, and shop. Yet the police department estimated that there were about 28 gambling joints in the District at the time.

Bea Kiyohara and the Northwest Asian American Theater

by Gary Iwamoto

Bea Kiyohara is best known in the community as the driving force behind the development of the Northwest Asian American Theater: the one who has spent the past 25 years dedicated to recognizing local Asian/Pacific American talent, bringing legitimate and innovative Asian/Pacific American drama to the stage in Seattle.

In the 1970s, the Seattle Chinatown/International District Preservation and Development Authority (PDA) was looking at projects to develop. Bea saw this as a perfect opportunity to realize her dream of a permanent performing home for theater and persuaded an appointment to the Board.

The PDA Board would spend long hours debating what was needed in the International District – more housing, more social services, more meal programs. Then Bea, who was quiet during most of the discussion, would say, "what about a theater. The responses of the tired board members ready to go home were, "Sure, Bea, anything you say."

Bea had her eye on an abandoned garage and car storage building owned by Dr. Toda. She approached the Wing Luke Asian Museum, which agreed to be a co-tenant. Under the leadership of McDonald Sullivan, Ben Woo, and Bob Santos, the PDA was able to convince the city of Seattle to provide seed money

for the design work. They also persuaded Rep. Gary Locke and the state legislature to approve a state construction bond to fund the majority of the renovation costs. Bea undertook a successful major capital campaign raising $75,000 from the community, foundation, and corporate

Bea Kiyohara. International Examiner file photo.

sources to equip and finish the structure as a working theater space. In 1981, Theater Off Jackson, home of the Northwest Asian American Theater, came into being.

Others helped, and perhaps someone else would have stepped in to take on the lead role had Bea not stuck with the idea of presenting plays and organizing the community, but let's give credit where credit's due. It was Bea who served for many years as the unpaid artistic director for the Northwest Asian American Theater. It was Bea who helped organize numerous progressive political shows uncovering the history of women and Japanese Americans in Washington. It was with Bea's encouragement that new works such as Nikki Nojima Louis' "Breaking the Silence,"

Bengie Santos' "Innovations," Ken Mochizuki's "Beacon Hill Boys," and "Miss Minidoka 1943," were developed and produced for the community. It was Bea who provided the forum for such talents as Leslie Ishii, Ken Mochizuki, Eddie Mui, Judi Nihei, and Gregg Hashimoto to try their hand at acting as a profession. It was Bea who nurtured the hidden performing itches of nonprofessional community folks such as Harry Fujita and Tama Tokuda to act on stage. It was Bea who encouraged the storyteller in Tomo Shoji and Bob Santos to create their own works for us to share.

Bea has earned the respect of other artistic organizations and leaders in these parts. She has acted with other major theaters such as the Seattle Repertory Theater, A Contemporary Theater, Seattle Children's Theater, and the Alice B. Theater. She currently serve on the Board of the Freehold Theater which runs an actor's training school. She has served as Chair of the King County Arts Commission.

With all of her community involvement, Bea also found time to pursue a career in education. While she was raising three kids, she worked full time as a counselor for the University of Washington's EOP program while pursuing a Master's Degree in Higher Education. She now has a Doctorate in Education and currently works at Seattle Central Community College where she started as a counselor and is now Dean of Student Development.

This article first appeared in the International Examiner, April 21 - May 5, 1999 issue.

Seattle Mayor Charlie Royer (front right) and city housing director, Ted Burton (front left) tour new housing projects in the International Disrict with Bob Santos (far right). International Examiner file photo.

Part Ten
The District Comes of Age

New Investments, New Immigrants Spur New Growth

In 1979 the Neighborhood Strategy Area (NSA) Program, a city-administered neighborhood revitalization supported by federal housing funds, began in the International District. The program called for housing renovation, business development, public improvements, and social service programs for low-income residents. Alan Kurimura, who was legislative assistant to City Council member George Benson and familiar with the District, was chosen to start the program. Though the program ended in 1983, its results were dramatic. The infusion of $4 million of city funds and nearly $2 million of federal funds leveraged $5 million private investment funds to rehabilitate seven commercial/residential buildings: Evergreen, Atlas, Freedman, Jackson, New Central, Leyte (renamed Far East), and Bush-Asia. Five of the buildings were privately owned. The renovations resulted in 283 new housing units and some 47,000 square feet of new commercial space for 50 businesses. The city also provided $1.7 million for District streetscaping - including new decorative lighting, sidewalks, and trees - to create an aesthetically pleasing residential environment.

The cost of renovating the District's old, run-down buildings was enormous. A single unit of housing (such as a studio or one bed-room unit) cost an average of $60,000 to renovate, more than it cost to build a new house. Though the city's decision to direct its resources to the District reflected its commitment to the area, it also reflected pressure from the community and the Asian American advocates inside city government. "The city has been doing more than just trying to establish better police relations in the International District," said Mayor Royer, referring to the District's perceived crime problem in the aftermath of the Wah Mee killings. "We made a commitment to this community six years ago that the city would provide whatever assistance was needed to make this area a good place to live and to run a business."

Many new small businesses also boosted commerce in the District. One successful example was the House of Hong. The elder Hong had operated the Atlas Restaurant in the Atlas Hotel building for several years. Starting as a single-counter operation, the restaurant later added an adjacent room with tables to accommodate its rapidly growing business, thus doubling its size. Unable to expand further at the Atlas building, the family purchased the building and property at Eighth and Jackson, which had been a Safeway supermarket in the 1940s and 50s and then an office furniture store. They then renovated the building and transformed it into a new restaurant. City staff Cindy Shinoda completed a Small Business Loan

Sculpture by George Tsutakawa. International Examiner file photo.

Bob Santos: Advisor, Confidant and Drinking Buddy for a Generation

by Gary Iwamoto

Luke Skywalker has his Obi Wan Kenobi. And when "Obi Wan" is translated from Jedi language into English, you find that: "Obi Wan" means "Uncle Bob." Bob Santos has fought the Evil Empire for more than 25 years and served as an advisor, mentor, confidante, and drink buddy for a generation of our community's Jedi Knights.

Born and raised a long, long time ago in, well, the International District, Uncle Bob has been a fighter all of his life. As a youth, he was a boxer, just like his dad, Sammy Santos. He was a Marine. And just when he was being sent to Korea during the Korean War, the truce was reached. They know that he was coming. Yes, even then, Uncle Bob was a peacemaker.

And when the 1960s came, Uncle Bob was on the front lines of the battle for civil rights. He served on the Seattle Human Rights Commission and began to forge harmonious working relationships outside of the Asian community. As Director of Project Caritas, Bob fought to provide positive opportunities for inner city youth.

Uncle Bob's role in revitalizing the International District is well-documented. As a kid growing up in Chinatown, Bob lived among the prostitutes, manongs, and transients, who, like the buildings, were often neglected and abandoned for this neighborhood.

The construction of Interstate 5 in the 1960s physically divided the area and churches. Families left Chinatown, moving into Beacon Hill and Rainier Valley. Closer to the commercial core, building were abandoned, some torn down for parking lots. The 1970s brought stricter building and fire

Bob Santos. International Examiner file photo.

codes that resulted in the closure and demolition of many buildings. The International District's population dropped substantially from 5000 in 1950 to 1300 in the 1970s. Businesses failed and buildings deteriorated. The construction of the Kingdome, beginning in 1972, generated traffic and parking problems. When Bob became the director of the International District Improvement Association (Inter*im)in 1972, the District had been in a steep decline.

Inter*im operated out of a small storefront on the corner of Maynard and Jackson in the old Bush Hotel. Under Uncle Bob's leadership, it became a haven for young activists, many of whom were recent college graduates or emerging professionals with fresh and innovative ideas toward serving the community (such as Bruce Miyahara, Theresa Fujiwara, Elaine Ikoma Ko, and Y.K.Kuniyuki). Plans were developed and proposals written to fund demonstration projects which would later become the International District Community Health Center, the Asian Counseling and Referral Service, the Denise Louie Education Center, and the International District Housing Alliance. Under Uncle Bob, Inter*Im sponsored a meal voucher program, a legal referral service/clinic, and a nutrition program. Inter*im also played a role in the development of the *International Examiner* through a Comprehensive Employment Training Act (CETA) grant for the paper's editor. Uncle Bob also wrote a regular column for the *Examiner* called "Inter*im's Corner."

One of Uncle Bob's proudest accomplishments as the director of Inter*im was the development of the Danny Woo International District Community Garden. The hillside between Washington and Main Street was overgrown with weeds and sticker bushes. Uncle Bob rallied a massive community effort to make the garden a reality. He negotiated lease agreements with the property owners, the Woo family, and the city of Seattle. He coaxed and cajoled the use of bulldozer and heavy machinery to remove the underbrush, persuaded the local horse racetrack to dump tons of horse manure to fertilize the land. He organized community work parties that brought in not only the young Asian activists but work crews from El Centro de la Raza and the United Indians for all Tribes. Uncle Bob instituted the annual community pig roast in the garden which continues today.

As director of Inter*im, Bob was instrumental in the formation of the public corporation today known as the Seattle Chinatown/International District Preservation and Development Authority, serving first as a board member and, later, executive director. Uncle Bob was instrumental in bringing badly needed housing to revitalize the District. Federal housing grants, low-interest loans, and partnership development agreements supported the rehabilitation of older apartments and hotels such as the Bush Hotel, the New Central Apartments, and the Jackson Apartments. Uncle Bob also laid the groundwork for the International District Village Square; he had the foresight more than 20 years ago to acquire the site, an abandoned bus maintenance and storage facility from Metro.

Aside from the District, Uncle Bob has had a tremendous impact on the lives of individuals. He is often cited as an employment reference for prospective job seekers, sometimes for applicants seeking the same job. His personal charm and easy going manner attracted people like Sue Taoka and Jeff Hattori to become involved with our community. When someone had problems dealing with the law or government bureaucracy, Uncle Bob was there to help. If he couldn't find a way to solve the problem, he'd be on the phone finding someone who could. As an aide to Congressman Mike Lowry and in his post as the Department of Housing and Urban Development's Secretary's Regional Representative for the Northwest Region, he made a career out of dealing with complaints by constituents.

If we were graded on what we do in life, Uncle Bob's report card would read, "works well with others." His relationships with other minority community leaders, particularly Bernie Whitebear, Roberto Maestas, and now King County Councilman Larry Gossett, were not only political alliances but strong friendships. The "Gang of Four" brought their communities together and developed a united stand on such diverse issues as fishing rights, immigrants' rights, welfare reform, and funding for social services.

Uncle Bob is dedicated without being dogmatic: an idealist with flexibility, hobnobbing with the political establishment without forgetting the little guy or gal..

*This article appeared in the International Examiner, April 21 - May 5, 1999 issue.

application for the Hongs, which was approved by the Federal Small Business Administration. Designer Joey Ing, an established restaurant architect, gave the eatery a contemporary design and decor. The restaurant was a huge success, attracting new customers to the District despite the negative publicity of the Wah Mee killings and a fire that closed the restaurant for a few months.

Perhaps the single largest factor contributing to the District's resurgence was the new wave of Asian immigration resulting from the Immigration and Naturalization Act of 1965. Under the Act, a limit of 170,000 immigrants from the Eastern Hemisphere was allowed to enter the United States annually, with a ceiling of 20,000 from each country. The 1965 Act eliminated prior quotas based on national origin and allowed substantially larger numbers of Asians to immigrate to the U.S. For example, the previous quota for Chinese immigration had been only 105, including overseas Chinese from Hong Kong, Singapore, France, Mexico, Canada, or any other country. While the population of the International District was about 1,700 in 1980, the Asian American population of Seattle grew from about 28,000 to about 44,000 during the 1970s, due mostly to the influx of new Asian immigrants. The flow of new immigration continued at a rate of some 2,000 annually to Washington throughout the next two decades. The dramatic increase in the Asian population, which has doubled each decade since 1970, greatly increased the demand for the Asian goods and services found in the District and played no small part in the revitalization of the area. In the last two decades, these recent Asian immigrants or refugees have started virtually every new business in the District.

International Examiner file photo.

In 1972, Sung Sook Choy, who had immigrated to Seattle a year earlier, opened what was probably the first Korean business in the District. Korean Food Production was a medium-sized grocery store which specialized in kim chee, Korean wonton, and rice cakes, and stocked a variety of canned goods. It also sold Korean records and 8-track tapes at its Sixth Avenue and Weller store. A couple of years later, a Korean restaurant opened at the Bush Asia Center, followed by the opening of the Korea Center building, which housed a market, the Seattle/Washington State Korean Association, and the Korean Community Services Center. Nevertheless, the Korean presence in the District has been small when compared with recent Chinese immigrants from Hong Kong and Taiwan, as well as Southeast Asian refugees.

The influx of refugees from Southeast Asia during the 1980s was dramatic. From "Operation Baby Lift" immediately after the fall of Saigon to 1990, the number of refugees in Washington State reached 50,000, the majority of them in King County. In September 1978, the first Vietnamese market in the District, the Thien-Thai Grocery Company, opened at Fifth and King. Huong Le, the owners' daughter, helped operate the store. "I have to order and go once a month to Los Angeles and San Francisco," she said at the time. "We want to see how business is going before we do direct importing." Two months later, the same owners opened a gift shop next door. In the early 1980s, Vietnamese opened the Asia BBQ and Fast Food on Jackson Street. It was one of the earlier Asian barbecue joints and the second Vietnamese business in the District. Across the street, Duc Tran opened another Vietnamese grocery called the Viet Hoa. Tran, a former counselor at the Employment Opportunity Center (an Asian/Pacific Islander job training and placement program), would eventually become a giant in the local supermarket industry, opening stores on upper Jackson Street and in Rainier Valley.

Before long, Vietnamese businesses - convenience stores, travel agencies, jewelry stores, hair salons, gift shops, apparel stores, and groceries - dominated Jackson Street from Fifth to Twelfth Avenues. They seemed to take every retail space that became available in the District, and created a demand for space at Twelfth and South Jackson, creating a commercial center now called "Little Saigon." Duc Tran began the move to that area when he took over a space that was once a furniture store and opened his Viet Wah supermarket and gift shop in the late 1880s. Soon after, developers were tearing down blocks of old, dilapidated wooden buildings that had stood vacant for decades and constructing new commercial buildings for new businesses. Now a four-block area, "Little Saigon" is a flourishing commercial center, an energetic extension of the International District.

As Vietnamese businesses sprouted up on Jackson Street, new Chinese businesses also emerged on King and Weller Streets during the past two decades. The construction of the Eng Association Building at Eighth and Weller and the renovation of the Tsue Chong Company across the street were major Chinese investments to the area. The Tsue Chong Company - established in 1912 and manufacturers of Chinese egg noodles, fortune cookies, and egg roll and wonton wrappers - is one of the older businesses in Chinatown. The renovations of the Ohio Hotel and Gee How Oak Tin Building in the late 1980s, the construction of a new building by the Dong family at Sixth Avenue and Maynard, and the renovation of the Rex and Eastern Buildings by Ray Chinn (with the help of Inter*Im) in the 1990s all added to the resurgence of the area.

Wards Cove Cannery Case Goes To Supreme Court

The Alaska Cannery Workers Association (ACWA), the brain child of Nemesio Domingo, made history when it filed class-action lawsuits, the first ever by a seasonal workforce, against three Alaska canneries for racial discrimination against Asian and Native Alaskan cannery workers. Nemesio, along with his younger brother Silme and a handful of others, created ACWA after the 1973 cannery season.

Always in the forefront of activism, Nemesio Domingo had started a progressive Filipino American newspaper, the Katipunan, while still a student at the University of Washington. Upon graduation, he worked with the state Department of Social and Health Services at the "Asian Desk," a position created to advise the department on how to improve services to Asian Americans. He left that position to start the Alaska Cannery Workers Association and to become more involved in the struggle against the Kingdome. The only protester arrested at the Kingdome groundbreaking ceremony, he was a key player in creating the Corrective Action Committee. The Committee advocated mitigating the stadium's impact, and persuaded the Cannery Workers Association to demand the hiring of Asian Americans in the stadium's construction. Again a visionary, Nemesio bought a new newspaper that was folding, the International Examiner, for a dollar and got people to develop it into a widely respected community newspaper.

But fighting discrimination was Domingo's main mission. A former cannery worker, he was instrumental in getting Asian American workers from ACWA, African American workers from the United Construction Workers Association, and Latino farm workers from the Northwest Chapter of the United Farmworkers of America to join forces to work for racial and economic justice. Together they formed the Northwest Labor Employment and Law Office (LELO).

Nemesio Domingo. International Examiner file photo.

In its early days, LELO focused on class-action lawsuits, and its lawyers filed a lawsuit in 1974 on behalf of the Asian and Native Alaskan cannery workers against Alaska canneries. The 1974 lawsuit was separated into three cases: Domingo v. New England Fish Company (NEFCO); Carpenter v. NEFCO-Fidalgo; and Atonio v. Wards Cove Packing Company.

In the lawsuits, the plaintiffs argued that the cannery companies maintained separate hiring channels for different jobs. Minority workers were recruited for unskilled cannery jobs from Alaska native villages and through the cannery union. Skilled and administrative jobs at the canneries were exclusively filled by whites, who received news of the job openings through word of mouth. The lack of posting for skilled positions and lack of a formalized promotion procedure, LELO argued, prevented minorities from advancement. Furthermore, companies provided segregated and inferior housing to minorities, cramming them together into filthy barracks-style bunkhouses, with little or no furniture and with inadequate facilities for washing and drying. Eating arrangements, the lawyers said, were also segregated with "Filipino" mess halls and "white" mess halls, and the disparities in the quality of food served resulted in food strikes by non-whites at the canneries. Rami Arditi, LELO's lawyer, also argued that non-whites were required to perform miscellaneous demeaning tasks such as cutting grass with hand sickles, machetes or sliming knives, cleaning under the dock and gathering empty cans out of the bay.

By 1984, after two courts made broad findings of discrimination in the lawsuits against New England Fish Company, the cannery workers settled the Domingo v. NEFCO and Carpenter v. NEFCO-Fidalgo lawsuits. Despite having the same arguments and legal underpinnings (and similar evidence) as the other two cases, the Wards

Ron Chew, the Master Educator

International Examiner and the Wing Luke Asian Museum

Ron Chew is both a savior and leader. His contributions to the District, and for that matter the entire country cannot be overstated. Intelligent, hard-working and suave, he has guided the makings of two prominent institutions into the community, the *International Examiner* and the Wing Luke Asian Museum. In the process he has educated the Asian Americans and others on what the International District and Asian Americans are all about.

Chew is the master educator who — as much as anyone — defined, promoted, and expressed the Asian American experience and pan-Asian Americanness.

A skilled journalist by training, it is likely that his biggest assets are his enthusiasm and dedication to the community and how he is able to recruit and involve people in community projects.

Chew's venture into journalism was rather abrupt.

He learned about discrimination, early and directly, while a student at the University of Washington. A conscientious journalism student, he spent hours at the library, reading newspapers around the country to sharpen his journalism skills. In addition, he was a proponent of diversifying the predominately white staff of *The Daily*, the university's student newspaper. After working as a top-notch reporter, he applied to be editor of the paper. When the editor job was given instead to a white women who hadn't even submitted an application for the position, Chew filed a racial discrimination suit, and won.

Meanwhile, Chew returned to his roots and got involved with the *International Examiner* newspaper upon graduation. Mayumi Tsutakawa was editor then, which was not too long after the Alaska Cannery Workers Association acquired the *Examiner* in 1974. When Tsutakawa left to take a job with the *Seattle Times* in the late 1970s, Chew assumed the duties of the editor.

Working for pennies, he put in long laborious hours. Able to recruit others, able to get others interested in working, able to guide and direct others, able to relate to the community, able to establish professionalism. He put it all together, writing articles, editing, assigning stories, soliciting staff, paste up, type set, layout, pick up and distribute paper. Wrote grants. Even did advertising.

Chew brought professionalism — a high standard of journalism — to a community paper, which the former head of the Seattle Public Library called the best in the state. More important, he captured and chronicled the important events, personalities, history, politics, arts, culture and issues of the International District and the broader Asian American communities. And he did so with a balanced approach.

Ron was the engine of the *Examiner* and without him, the paper would have failed long ago.

After a decade as editor, Chew left the paper but not the community. In 1991, he took over the reins of the Wing Luke Asian Museum and, within a year, turned a struggling operation into a vibrant, bustling community institution.

In the early days the museum, which is named after Seattle's first Asian American elected official, focused largely on the Chinese American community, folk art and culture, and traditions of Asian countries. Chew changed the focus of the museum so that it would concentrate more on the pan-Asian American experience, and to educate us of the stories, the experience and inner emotion, feelings, attitude of all Asian American groups. Furthermore, engaging the participation of the community in planning, designing, and providing information, artifacts and photos for the exhibits became as important as the final product itself.

His first major exhibit was named "Executive Order 9066: 50 Years Before and 50 Years After," and covered the history of Japanese Americans in Seattle. It opened some 50 years after the signing of the infamous order that interned that group. The highly successful exhibit had the help of some 100 volunteers, who helped build (among other things) a replica of a typical barrack housing at Minidoka.

A couple of years later, the museum highlighted the "Fall of Saigon and Aftermath," an exhibit about the Vietnamese American community which was also highly celebrated.

Exhibits on other Asian American groups such as the Koreans and Chinese have followed while "One Song, Many Voices: The Asian Pacific American Experience" has been the museum's main exhibit. Other major exhibits at the museum include a display on the International District, Filipino artists in the Northwest, garment workers, musicians, photographers and artists.

"Wing Luke is a wonderful model," said Claudine Brown, the arts program director for the Nathan Cummings Foundation. "What the Wing Luke has done is to make the entire community the stakeholders. It was a real revolutionary act in the museum field to give the community that much say".[1]

Chew believes the WLAM should be an ecomuseum. "Unlike traditional museums, ecomuseums make the past relevant to current social issues," he said. It links the past with the present and the future, and it extends our mission from gathering things to being a progressive force and not just a silent witness".[2]

"In most museums, the community is on an advisory board; we see the museum as an advisory board to the community," Chew said. "We see ourselves very much in the middle of the fray, championing issues, and using history to correct injustices." "We have the makings of a real powerful museum that's never been done anywhere else," he said of the only pan-Asian American museum in the country. Becoming a national model of things to come.

Chew received the Governor's Heritage Award from the Washington State Arts Commission, the Distinguished Service Award from the National Association of Asian American Studies and was awarded the prestigious National Award for Museum Service. In 2000, he was appointed to the National Council on the Humanities by President Clinton.

1. Ferdinand M. de Leon, "Wing Luke Asian Museum Coming of Age," *Seattle Times*, June 22, 1997, Section L pages 1 and 2.
2. Ibid.

Cove case took a different path of dubious historic distinction in the annals of America's civil right cases.

In 1983, federal District Court Judge Quackenbush ruled in favor of Ward's Cove Company. A three-judge panel in the Ninth Circuit Court of Appeals upheld his decision in 1985. Both decisions, however, ignored the 1971 Griggs standard set by the Supreme Court in Griggs v. Duke Power Company. The Griggs standard recognized "disparate impact" - i.e., "practices that are fair in form but discriminatory in practice" - and required employers to prove that their actions were justified by business necessity. The Wards Cove workers appealed to a nine-judge panel of the Ninth Circuit Court. In 1987, that panel of judges rebuked Judge Quackenbush and the three-judge panel, and upheld the Griggs standard. The Wards Cove Packing Company then appealed to the U.S. Supreme Court.

In 1989, Atonio v. Wards Cove went to the highest court in the land. Arguing the case for the cannery workers was Arditi. Seated next to him was Bill Lann Lee, who would become the Assistant Attorney General for Civil Rights under the Clinton Administration. Lee, then the senior attorney for the NAACP Legal Defense Fund, had filed a friend of the courts brief in support of the cannery workers' case. The Supreme Court at the time was controlled by a conservative majority with the addition of new judges appointed by Presidents Reagan and Bush. In a landmark civil rights decision, the Supreme Court retreated from the previously-held Griggs standard, in a divisive 5-4 decision. They narrowed the definition of "disparate impact" and placed the burden of proof upon the workers to show that discrimination was a direct result of the employer's actions. The case was sent back to the Federal District Court, which found the Wards Cove

Rep. Norm Mineta (right) with U.S. Attorney General Dick Thornburgh after the presentation of the first redress checks. International Examiner file photo.

Packaging Company innocent of intentional discrimination under the new standard.

The Supreme Court decision on the Wards Cove case was a huge setback for racial minorities; it followed other decisions by the high court that turned back the clock on civil rights in America. In a minority opinion, Supreme Court Justice Stevens wrote that the Wards Cove cannery "bears an unsettling resemblance to aspects of a plantation economy."

Meanwhile, to help strengthen civil right laws which were weakened because of Wards Cove and other Supreme Court decisions, Congress passed the Civil Rights Act of 1991. The Act attempted to reinstate the Griggs model of adverse impact and to make it easier for employees to file discrimination suits against employers. However, after

Ward's Cove spent $175,000 in lobbying efforts, Alaska Senators Frank Murkowski and Ted Stevens brokered a deal with the Act's sponsors to exempt Wards Cove - and only Wards Cove - from the new law. The sponsors of the Act believed the support of the two Alaska Senators was needed in order for the bill to pass. Community members, however, were outraged. "This is like saying everyone can sit in the front of the bus except for Rosa Parks," said Gloria Caoile, of the Asian Pacific Heritage Council. In the following legislative session, Representative Jim McDermott (D-Wash.) from Seattle introduced the Justice for Ward's Cove Workers Act to repeal the exemption in the 1991 Civil Rights Act. Senators Edward Kennedy (D-Mass.) and Patty Murray (D-Wash.) introduced a companion bill in the Senate. With Republican control of both houses, the bills did not move.

Finally, on August 7, 2000, 50 people packed the small courtroom in the Federal Courthouse in downtown Seattle to hear oral arguments in the Wards Cove v. Atonio case. The hearing was the result of the latest appeal by workers to reinstate the Griggs standard and resolve the case. Many of the plaintiffs were in their early 20s when they first filed the Wards Cove case; now in their 40s and 50s, they were joined by a new generation of activists. To date, the case is unresolved.

Redress for Japanese Americans[1]

On October 14, 1990, a standing-room-only crowd packed the Nisei Veterans Hall. They were there to witness the historic presentation of a letter of apology and $20,000 to the five oldest Seattle Japanese Americans entitled to redress compensation. For local activists, the event marked the closing of a long battle (which began in Seattle's International District) to recognize the hardship and losses suffered by Japanese American communities due to their unjust World War II internment. The redress issue first arose in 1970, when a resolution in support of redress was placed before the Japanese Americans Citizens League (JACL) national convention. Although the resolution passed, as did similar ones in 1972 and 1974, little was done; there was no consensus nationally, within JACL or the Japanese American community, on the wisdom of redress. The Seattle JACL chapter, however, was steadfast about redress and established the Seattle Evacuation Redress Committee.

The committee was headed by Henry Miyatake, who had researched the internment issue for years, and included Shosuke Sasake, Mike Nakata, Chuck Kato, and Ken Nakano. After months of study and preparation, the committee developed a specific proposal for redress which included monetary compensation. Although the proposal languished in the national JACL, the Seattle chapter convinced President Gerald Ford to revoke Executive Order 9066 (which had never been rescinded) in 1976 and to call the internment a "a national mistake." The Seattle chapter then polled JACL members nationally and found that 94 percent favored mandating payments to internees. In 1978, they persuaded the national organization's Committee for Redress to propose such a plan. A year later, Representative Mike Lowry (D- Seattle), submitted the first redress bill, developed with the local JACL's Seattle Evacuation Committee through Ruthann Kurose, Lowry's staff person. He introduced the bill, which called for $15,000 for individual compensation (plus per diem), to the House on November 28, 1979. The bill languished in committee and died. Meanwhile, having to choose whether to pursue legislation for redress or the establishment of a commission to develop findings and make recommendations, the Committee for Redress chose the latter -much to the disappointment of the Seattle chapter.

Subsequently, a bill was submitted and passed in Congress to establish a Commission on Wartime Relocation and Internment of Civilians. The commission traveled from city to city gathering heart-wrenching testimony about the incarceration's effects on Japanese Americans. Based on the Commission's recommendations, Representative Lowry introduced his second redress bill in June of 1983 with 44 co-sponsors. However, when House Majority Leader Representative Jim Wright and Representative Norman Mineta introduced House Bill HR 4110, the Civil Liberties Act of 1983, Lowry convinced the co-sponsors of his bill to sign

on to that bill. The Civil Liberties Act of 1983 was presented to the House with 74 co-sponsors on October 6 of that year, calling for acceptance of the findings and recommendations of the Commission on Wartime Relocation and Internment of Citizens. Unfortunately, neither that bill nor a similar bill presented in the Senate moved out of their respective committees. Redress bills were reintroduced in the House and Senate again in 1983 and two years later, but those also failed.

Meanwhile, the Seattle JACL chapter led the way in obtaining monetary compensation for Japanese Americans who lost jobs locally with the Seattle School District, the state of Washington, and the city of Seattle due to internment. The Seattle JACL was able to garner key support from elected officials and staff. School Board member

T.J.Vasser was instrumental in getting the School District's approval. Senator George Flemming introduced the bill in the State Senate, while House members Gary Locke and Art Wang ushered in legislation that enabled the allocation of state funds for compensation.

Finally, in 1987, House Majority Leader Tom Foley (D-Spokane) introduced the final redress bill with 125 co-sponsors; Senator Sparky Matsunaga (D-Hawaii) introduced it in the Senate with 75 co-sponsors, and the bill finally passed. The redress, authorized by the Civil Liberties Act of 1988, came almost 50 years after the 120,000 persons of Japanese ancestry were removed from the West Coast and placed in internment camps. The Act provided $20,000 to every living internee and a public education fund to "prevent recurrence of any similar

New Uwajimaya Village complex. Eugene Tagawa photo.

event." It was an especially great victory for the Seattle JACL, who had led the charge.

Development Booms in the 1990s

The 1990s were boom years for development in Seattle's south downtown. Among the jewels in the District's crown was the $21 million International District Village Square project, the largest public-private development in the neighborhood's history. Completed in 1997, the Village Square was an innovative, intergenerational, multi-use facility with housing for the elderly. Social service agencies were also housed in the building to serve residents and the Asian/Pacific Islander community at large. The Village Square was considered a national model of community development and was extensively studied by other communities around

the country. Future plans for Village Square include a second compound across the street. This compound will contain a city-operated gym and a branch public library on the ground floor, office space for social service agencies on the second floor, underground parking, and some 50 family units on the upper floors. The Village Square project and Nikkei Manor (a new assisted living facility for Japanese American elderly with retail commercial space at street level) were the first new developments on South Dearborn Street, the southern border of the District, in decades. At the north end of the District, just east of the freeway on Jackson Street, the new Pacific Rim Center -a retail/residential complex - was constructed along a steep hillside that had never been built on before. The project, completed in 2000, boosted activity on upper Jackson Street and helped connect the International District with Little Saigon.

In 1996, when the decision to build a new stadium for the Seattle Mariners was announced, the District more or less took the news in stride; the same happened for the announcement of a new football stadium for the Seattle Seahawks a couple of years later. Although the sites for the new stadiums were not determined right away, everyone knew that they would most likely be near the old Kingdome, next to the District. The muted response, less dramatic than earlier decades, might have been expected. The District had generally become accustomed to having a 65,000-seat stadium nearby and to the traffic and parking problems caused during event days. Moreover, the District had developed important mechanisms to control land use through the Special Review Board, so there was less concern about being overtaken by parking lots, motels, and fast food places. A merchants-controlled nonprofit parking association had been developed under the leadership of Glenn Chinn to help direct and manage parking. The District had also established viable entities like the Public Development Authority to develop needed housing for the poor, elderly and others as well as other community facilities to help preserve its historic character.

While large-scale protests were virtually absent, the District was still concerned over renewed property speculation, traffic congestion, loss of business during events, and public safety. Yet unlike two decades earlier, the developer listened to and worked with the District to mitigate the impacts. First and Goal, Inc., the developer of the stadium for football team owner Paul Allen, was particularly willing to work with the District as well as the Pioneer Square and South Downtown Industrial Area. At the urging of Sue Taoka of the Public Development Authority

New development at the Union Station property on Fifth Avenue. Eugene Tagawa photo.

Uwajimaya

Fujimatsu Moriguchi immigrated to Seattle in 1923. He worked as a fish cutter at Main Fish Company to learn fish production. Five years after he arrived, the elder Moriguchi purchased a truck and started a business in Tacoma selling fishcakes out of his truck store. He named the business Uwajimaya after the name of his hometown in Japan. The family lost the business during World War II when they were forced into internment camp.

After the war, the Moriguchis moved to Seattle and in 1945 opened a small fish market at Fourth and Main. Over the years, authentic Japanese food and gifts items were added to store product lines.

During the Seattle World's Fair in 1962, the elder Moriguchi opened a successful Japanese gift shop at the fair. That same year, he died, leaving the business to his sons Kenzo, Tomio, Akira and Toshi. The sons subsequently divided ownership shares with their mother and three sisters. Inheriting their father's zeal, the sons took over the business operations and expansion.

In 1968, a branch was opened at Southcenter Shopping Center. Two years later, the small store on Main Street was moved to a much larger, newly-constructed building on Sixth Avenue South, between King and Weller Streets. The new supermarket/gift shop quickly outgrew itself and, in 1978, a $1.75 million expansion of the building was added. That same year, another branch of Uwajimaya was opened on the Eastside at an old Safeway site at Northeast 24th Avenue in Bellevue.

Meanwhile, as the demand for Asian products continued to grow, the sons established their own import business called SeaAsia, a wholesale business that produces rice, tofu, and other Asian food items and products. The Asian supermarket chain has stores in Bellevue and Beaverton, Oregon, which sell food and

Tomio Moriguchi. Examiner file photo.

goods from Japan, Korea, China, and Philippines. To date the chain is expected to generate some $30 million total in annual revenues from the three stores.

Tomio Moriguchi is currently the president and chief executive officer of Uwajimaya. Since the 1960s, he has been active in the District and played a major role in the development and operations of the International District Improvement Association (Inter*Im), the now-defunct International District Economic Association (IDEA), Merchants Parking Association and Chinatown/International District Public Development Authority. In the late 1980s, he was instrumental in creating the Chinatown/International District Business Improvement Area (BIA), which is designed to promote area businesses, and has played an active role in that organization since its inception. Moriguchi has also been active with the Japanese American Citizens League and Nikkei Concerns, which established (and now operates) a nursing home and other programs for the Japanese American elderly.

In 2000, Uwajimaya received the University of Washington School of Business Bradford Award, which honors one of the state's top minority-owned businesses.

A new Uwajimaya Village, a joint development of Uwajimaya, Inc. and Lorig Associates, was completed in November 2000. It includes over 70,000 square feet of retail space anchored by the Uwajimaya Asian food and gift market, 176 apartments, and 360 parking spaces. The grocery and gift shop is the largest Asian supermarket in North America. The new tenants include Kinokuniya Books, Chinoise Sushi Bar & Asian Grill, Washington Mutual Bank, Yuriko's Cosmetics, Tully's Coffee, Honeymoon Teas, Yummy House Bakery, and several small Asian bistros such as Shilla's Korean BBQ, Saigon Bistro, Thai Place and Inay's Filipino Kitchen.

Uwajimaya Village contains public artworks, including a fountain by Seattle sculptor George Tsutakawa, a lantern standing 20 feet high and weighing some 18 tons, a 23-foot tall copper dragon, and the International District's ornamental light poles.

(and others in the community), Democrat State Representatives Velma Veloria and Dawn Mason inserted a special provision in the legislation which provided for the stadium's construction. According to this provision, First and Goal, Inc. had to provide $10 million to mitigate the stadium's impact on its surrounding neighborhoods. Eventually, a South Downtown Foundation was established with some $600,000 to leverage and provide funds to the adjacent neighborhoods for marketing, preserving, and enhancing economic and community improvements in these areas.

Also in the 1990s, demand for office space in downtown Seattle skyrocketed, driven by the growth of the high-tech industry. Vacancy rates were an unprecedented 2 percent or less. With the exception of the area around Union Station, adjacent to the western border of the District, there was very little vacant land. Union Station was a railway terminal originally built in 1910 and listed on the National Historic Register. Since it stopped being a train station after the Union Pacific discontinued its service to Union Station in 1971, there had been periodic attempts to redevelop the property. On one occasion, the Port of Seattle explored the property as an inter-modal transportation center and, on another occasion, as a terminal for Greyhound and other bus lines. Both ideas met strong resistance from the International District. Then, in 1984, Union Pacific, who then owned the property and adjacent land, introduced a new development which departed from all predecessors. It was an extroverted concept which concentrated on improving Union Station access for all modes of circulation; it was also consistent with the development goals of adjacent neighborhoods. Working with the International District and Pioneer Square, the city

drew up an acceptable Planned Unit Development (PUD) for the Union Station area which allowed for commercial buildings and required the construction of parking facilities, open space, pedestrian paths and other amenities. In 1990, a master use permit was issued to Nitze-Stagen, the developer of the Union Station properties.

Some 10 years later, much of the Union Station properties have been built, and a two to three block area - vacant and abandoned for nearly a century - has been dramatically transformed. Union Station itself, an 80,000-square-foot renovation costing $30 million, was completed in 2000, along with four new office buildings and a parking facility. Paul Allen, Microsoft co-founder and multi-billionaire owner of the Seattle Seahawks, constructed one of the four buildings (an 11-story office complex containing some 310,000 square feet) immediately south of the Union Station Building. Allen's purpose was to consolidate his management company, Vulcan Northwest, which occupies the top five floors. His ultra-contemporary building, simply called 505 Union Station, features a series of slanted glazed-glass windows and a "waterfall wall" on the north side. Just behind Paul Allen's building, Opus (a leading commercial building developer) constructed the Opus Center with three buildings: Opus East, Opus West and Opus South. However, most of the space in these buildings is leased to Amazon.com, whose headquarters is a short distance away on North Beacon Hill.

With the Union Station properties and the construction of the new two-block Uwajimaya Village across the street, Fifth Avenue South now rivals King and Jackson Streets as the busiest street in the District.

The Lane Street Controversy

The battle over the District's name and identity has continued for years and shows no sign of stopping. It is an internal struggle and a divisive issue, reflecting persistent inter- and intra-ethnic differences within the neighborhood. Some in the Chinese community, including the Chinese/Chinatown Chamber of Commerce and Chong Wa, have insisted that the name "Chinatown" be used or at least included, as in "Chinatown/International District." They say the name should be used because that is what most local

Lane Street protesters gather at Chong Wah. Examiner file photo.

people call the area; many in the business sector believe it is a name familiar to tourists that will attract business.

On the other hand, there are those who say Chinatown or the Chinese sector, like Japantown, is part of the area but not the entire area. This group of pan-ethnic, younger, progressive, Americanized District activists and workers assert that using "Chinatown" or even "Chinatown/International District" does not describe the area in its complexity. The term fails to recognize the existence of other sectors -such as the Japanese, Vietnamese and Filipinos, and for that matter the whites, American Indians, and African Americans who have always been in the area. Chinatown centers on King and Weller Streets and comprises some eight blocks in the center of the 40 blocks commonly known as the International District. These pan-Asian Americans want to see the area, including the Chinatown sector, developed as an Asian American neighborhood serving as a regional commercial and cultural center for all Asian Americans. They agree that the name can be misleading and vague - for instance, "International" connotes "foreign" or "not American" - but "International" is still the term that seems to best represent the District's diversity.

In the spring of 1998 Uwajimaya, the huge regional supermarket/gift shop headquartered in the District, announced a plan for a major expansion that set the community buzzing with controversy. The plan called for the construction of a new complex, Uwajimaya Village (immediately south of the existing building), and the relocation of the supermarket, gift store, and bookstore from the existing site, and new retail and restaurants on the ground floor. The upper floors would contain some 177 new apartments. A new underground parking facility would be constructed under the supermar-

ket/apartment complex with an adjoining new ground level parking lot developed on the adjacent block. Lane Street, which adjoins the parking lot and the supermarket, would have to be vacated or closed.

Shortly thereafter, members of the Chong Wa Association and Chinese/Chinatown Chamber of Commerce learned of the project in a local daily newspaper article. They began an organized campaign against it. Called "Save Lane Street," the two organizations mounted an all-out attempt to curtail the project by disallowing the street vacation. Over the next few months, they organized mass demonstrations around Uwajimaya, submitted a petition with hundreds of signatures to the City Council, lobbied city council members, and filed lawsuits and appeals to block the vacation of Lane Street. The two primary spokespersons for the campaign were May Wan and Ted Choi. The group argued that the Environment Impact Statement was inadequate, that the time allowed for comment on the project was too short, that the scale of the project would cause traffic and parking problems, and adversely affect existing businesses. They also complained that closing Lane Street would limit access for emergency vehicles, and that a private business or individual should not be allowed to secure a street vacation.

Most people in and out of the community actually supported the project, which would develop a couple of blighted blocks into a new complex that would create more jobs, businesses, and much needed housing. Street vacations in Seattle are not uncommon. For many, especially those who wanted to see greater development in the District, vacating a block of Lane Street- largely unused and abandoned for decades - was a good exchange for the planned Uwajimaya Village project and the new development it

would bring. Even the "Save Lane Street" group claimed that they were in favor of the new project; they simply opposed the closure of Lane Street, or so they said.

The uproar over the project by the "Save Lane Street" side seemed to reflect the old animosity and inter-ethnic conflict that has existed in the District for years. Businesses in the District welcome the patronage of those of a different ethnic or racial group, but business competition can sometimes lead to racial or ethnic conflicts. The fact that only the Chinese protested against the Uwajimaya Village project suggests that ethnicity had something to do with it. The closure of Lane Street, traffic problems, and other complaints about the project may well have been a pretext for shielding larger issues of territorial dominance and control of the area, and concern that the project would detract from their businesses.

For better or worse, the City Council approved the street vacation and the Uwajimaya Village complex was built. Sadly, though, the Lane Street issue renewed ethnic conflict and animosity between the Chinese and others in the area, which still lingers.

Rebuffing the Big Mac Attack

Indeed, on the heels of the "Save Lane Street" strife came the McDonald's controversy. In the early spring of 2000, rumors were confirmed that McDonald's was negotiating with the owner of the Buty Building, which sits on the western entrance to the District. The building's owner was Michael Chu, who also owned other property and a business in the District. He was also a supporter of the "Save Lane Street" campaign. Activists in the area - especially those who advocated for a pan-Asian American district

- became concerned that a multinational corporation like McDonald's would dilute the unique historical and cultural qualities of the area. Chong Wa and the Chinese/Chinatown Chamber of Commerce, of which Michael Chu was a member, argued that the property owner had the right to lease to anyone, and that protesting McDonald's as a new business in the area was discriminatory. In response to the Special Review District's goal of preserving Asian character of the District, Chu's response was "what is Asian?" McDonald's argued that there were McDonald's in San Francisco's Chinatown, Hawaii, China and Japan. "We can and have adapted to Asian taste and culture," said McDonald's representatives.

Those opposed to McDonald's said that McDonald's simply does not fit in what is the most Asian ethnic neighborhood in the Northwest. They added that McDonald's was insensitive to the Asian American community and the District's desire to maintain and preserve its historic and unique Asian character. "Fatty hamburgers, French fries, Egg McMuffins, and other foods and drinks served at a McDonald's are not part of the Asian palate. In addition, there are very few families with children living in the area and the largest population in the District, the Asian elderly, are certainly not interested to going to McDonald's for a Big Mac or Egg McMuffin. So, what benefit is there in having a McDonald's to the area?" They also said a McDonald's attracts loiterers and littering, which they believed would exacerbate public safety concerns and sanitation problems at a key location in the District.

The District activists were not alone in their opposition to McDonald's. Mayor Paul Schell sent a letter to McDonald's early on,

urging them not to open in the District. "A McDonald's just doesn't fit in that neighborhood," he said, echoing the words of the activists. A large number of Asian American, community, and labor groups opposed a McDonald's in the International District, including the International District Housing Alliance, International District Improvement Association, Inter*Im Community De-

Protest against McDonalds.
International Examiner file photo.

velopment Association, Organization of Chinese Americans, Chinese Information and Service Center, Minority Executive Directors' Coalition, Northwest Labor Employment and Law Office, Commission on Asian Pacific American Affairs, and Asian Pacific American Labor Alliance. Many area businesses as well as individuals, including elected officials such as King County Councilmember Larry Gossett, and State

Representatives Velma Veloria, Sharon Tomiko Santos, and Kip Tokuda, also urged McDonald's to stay away.

Three months after the campaign against McDonald's began, some 100 protesters demonstrated at a downtown McDonald's. McDonald's then decided to withdraw its effort to enter the International District. The company's decision, the activists said, had nothing to do with becoming sensitive or respectfully preserving the ethnic character of the area. Evidently, Don Becka, McDonald's Regional Real Estate Manager, was concerned about the strength and size of the opposition and demonstrations aimed at the fast food chain, and rightly so. The demonstration on June 22 at the Third and Pine Street restaurant was just the beginning of a comprehensive campaign to include more demonstrations, boycotts, media campaigns, and other strategies to damage McDonald's image.

A week after McDonald's decided to pull out, the Seattle City Council wrote a letter to McDonald's thanking them for doing so. "We believe that this decision will benefit this neighborhood in a number of ways, most significantly by helping to retain the International District's unique historical character and allowing for continued support of its residents, small business owners, and non-profit agencies," they wrote.

"McDonald's decision not to locate in the International District was a major victory for all of us who want to preserve the historical pan-Asian character of the area and to make it a safe place to live, shop, visit and work," the activists wrote in a statement to the press. "It is a win for the International District community, neighborhood self-determination, cultural pluralism, historical preservation, diversity, and a progressive Seattle."

A Changing Pan-Asian American Community

At the end of the 1980s, the census counted some 1,735 persons living in the International District. Some 47 percent were Asian Americans, 39 percent White, 10 percent African American, and 2 percent Native American. Male residents continued to outnumber women 2 to 1. However, the overall population of the area has become younger as the elderly population (60 years and older) decreased to 44 percent, after being the majority for several decades. In 1990, Asian Americans comprised 55 percent, Whites 36 percent, African-Americans 5 percent and Native Americans 3 percent of the District's population. Over half of the population was 60 years and older. Among the Asians, 62 percent were elderly. In 1989, the median income of single persons was $5,589 and some $10,147 for households of two or more persons. In comparison, the city's median income for single persons was $20,976 and $29,353 for households. By 1995, Asian Americans comprised some 16 percent of the city's population (85,140), according to official state estimates. The number of Asian Americans in King County, of which Seattle is the largest city, reached an estimated 168,556 or 10 percent of the county's total population, up from 7.68 percent in 1990. About half of all Asian Americans in the state resided in the County.

While Chinatowns, Japantowns, Koreatowns, and Manilatowns in other cities struggle to survive, the International District perseveres with a new vitality. At the turn of the new century, the District's population is over 2000 persons (and growing), with an emerging middle class that includes an increasing number of white professionals. With the addition of more family hous-

The International District today with the International District Village Square complex (center front). Intenational Examiner file photo.

ing, the neighborhood's diversity will continue to grow.

Today, the International District remains one of a very few distinctly ethnic neighborhoods in the city. It has refused to fade away or be assimilated. Its place as a home for Asian immigrants and elderly, organizations, and business continues. As a regional base for Asian goods and services, it has never been stronger. It is a place where the pan-Asian American neighborhood grows, struggles, and changes without compromising its integrity as an Asian American community: a place where the confluence of Asian and Asian American culture and ideology clumsily met, clashed, and in turn awkwardly merged with urban America.

The recent resurgence of the District has brought physical improvements and a new social order. Middle-income people can now find adequate housing in the area along with the elderly and poor. A new political structure with progressive leadership from both the business and non-profit communities has essentially replaced the influence of traditional groups. Pan-ethnic leadership and thinking, with respect for diversity, has emerged, while some traditional groups based on a single ethnic interest still persevere. Through political action and care, the International District is no longer an isolated, neglected neighborhood. Rather, the District has become wholesomely integrated with its adjacent neighbors while preserving its unique Asian American identity.

Notes to Parts

Part 1/Seattle's First Chinese Settlement

1. Lucile McDonald, "Seattle's First Chinese Resident," Seattle Times Sunday Magazine, September 11, 1955, p. 5.
2. Clarence B. Bagley, History of Seattle from the Earliest Settlement to the Present Time, Chicago: S.J. Clarke Company, 1916, p. 173.
3. Willis Sayres, This City of Ours, Seattle, 1936, p. 37.
4. David Buerge, Seattle in the 1880s; The Historical Society of Seattle and King County: Seattle, 1986, p. 107.

Part 2/The Anti-Chinese Movement in Washington

1. W.P. Wilcox, "Anti-Chinese Riots in Washington," Washington Historical Quarterly, Vol. XX, Seattle, 1929, pp. 204-212.
2. Robert E. Wynne, Reaction to the Chinese in the Pacific Northwest and British Columbia: 1850 to 1910, Arno Press, 1978, p.84.
3. Kurt E. Armbruster, Orphan Road: The Railroad Comes to Seattle, 1853-1911. Washington State University Press: Pullman, Washington, 1999, p.53.
4. Richard McDonald and Lucile McDonald, The Coals of Newcastle: A Hundred Years of Hidden History. Issaquah Alps Trail Club: 1982, pp. 35-36.
5. Robert C. Nesbit, Thomas Burke: He Built Seattle, Seattle: University of Washington Press, 1961, p. 110.
6. Ibid, p. 200.
7. John C. Shideler, Coal Towns in the Cascades, Spokane: Melior Publications, 1986, pp. 35-37.

Part 3/Nihonmachi (Japantown)

1. Kazuo Ito, Issei: A History of Japanese Immigrants to North America. Seattle: Executive Committee for Publication of Issei, pp. 780-81 and Ronald E. Magden, Furusato: Tacoma-Pierce County Japanese. Tacoma: Tacoma Japanese Community Service, 1998, pp. 3-16.
2. Ibid, p. 781.
3. "Seattle Ministerial Federation Report of the Committee on Orientals," June 4, 1917.
4. Bill Hosokawa, Nisei: The Quiet Americans. New York: William Morrow and Company, 1969.
5. Seattle Buddhist Temple Archives pamphlet (undated).
6. Frank Miyamoto, "An Immigrant Community in America," in Hilary Conroy and T. Scott Miyakawa, East Across the Pacific. Santa Barbara: CLIO Press, 1972, p. 235.
7. Ito, Issei, pp. 292-93.
8. Robert A. Wilson and Hosokawa, East to America: A History of the Japanese in the United States. New York: William Morrow and Company, 1980, p. 72.
9. Ibid, p. 68.
10. Gene Viernes, "Sliming and Butchering Fish in the Alaska Canneries," International Examiner, March 1977.
11. Ito, Issei, p.353.
12. Wilson and Hosokawa, East to America, p. 69.

Part 4/From Sojourners to Settlers

1. Guimary and Masson, "The Exploitation of Chinese Labor in the Alaska Salmon Industry," Chinese America: History and Perspectives. Chinese Historical Society of America: 1990, pp. 91-106.
2. Life History of Mr. Woo Gen, July 29, 1924, p.16, Survey of Race Relations, Stanford University, Hoover Institution Archives. Quoted in Ronald Takaki, Strangers From A Different Shore, New York: Penguin Books, 1989, p. 125.

Part 5/Filipinos Arrive in the District

1. Fred Cordova, Filipinos: Forgotten Asian Americans, Seattle: Demonstration Project for Asian Americans, p. 1.
2. Sucheng Chan, Asian Americans: An Interpretive History. Boston: Twayne Publishers, 1991, pp. 16-17.
3. Violet Rabaya, "Filipino Immigration: The Creation of a New Social Problem" in Roots: An Asian American Reader, eds. Amy Tachiki, Ed Wong, Franklin Odo with Buck Wong. Los Angeles: UCLA Asian American Studies Center, 1971.
4. Cordova, Filipinos, p. 9.
5. Takaki, Strangers, p.315
6. Cordova, Filipinos, p. 177.
7. Nancy Koslosky, "Filipinos in Washington, Part 1," International Examiner, June 1976.
8. Cordova, Filipinos, p. 20.
9. Sebastian Abella, Filipino Forum, April 1929.
10. Richard C. Berner, Seattle 1921-1941: From Boom To Bust. Seattle: Charles Press, 1991, p. 211.
11. Helen Zia, Asian American Dreams: The Emergence of an Asian American People. New York: Farrar, Strauss, and Giroux, 2000, p. 142.

12. Richard C. Berner, Seattle 1921-1940: From Boom to Bust. Seattle: Charles Press: 1992, p. 391.
13. Ibid, p.391.
14. Zia, Asian American, p.145.
15. Berner, Seattle, p.190-191.
16. Gene Viernes, "Union Ends Reign of Cannery Contractors," International Examiner, May/June 1977.

Part 6/From the Heydays of the 1920s through the Depression

1. Paul de Barros, Jackson Street After Hours: The Roots of Jazz in Seattle. Sasquatch Books, Seattle, 1993, pp. 2-3.
2. Ibid, p. 23.
3. Ibid, p. 30.
4. see Paul de Barros, Jackson Street After Hours: The Roots of Jazz in Seattle, Sasquatch Books, Seattle, 1993.
4. Berner, Seattle 1921-1940, p. 212.
5. Frank Miyamoto, Social Solidarity Among the Japanese in Seattle, University of Washington pubication in Social Sciences,

December, 1939.
6. David Berner, Seattle 1921-1940, p. 212.

Part 7/Japanese American Removal and Incarceration

1. Herbert Hill, Anti-Oriental agitation and the rise of working-class racism, Society, Jan/Feb. 1973, pp. 43-63.

Part 8/International District Emerges After World War II

1. Terrin Haley, "Orient Expressed," Seattle Weekly, June 22, 1988, p. 26.
2. Howard Droker, "Seattle Race Relations during the Second World War," Pacific Northwest Quarterly, October 1976.
3. "Tales of the I.D.," Seattle Times, February 27, 1994, Section L, pp. 1-4.
4. S. Frank Miyamoto and Robert W. O'Brien, "A Survey of Some Changes in the Seattle Japanese Community since Evacuation," Research Studies of the State College of

Washington, June 1947.
5. de Barros, p.80.
6. de Barros, pp.80-81.
7. Seattle Times, June 24, 1951, p. D6.

Part 9/The District Battles Hard Times

1. Ron Chew, Reflections of Seattle's Chinese Americans, Seattle: University of Washington Press and Wing Luke Museum, 1994, p. 115.
2. Peter Rinearson, "Chow faces defections among Chinese-Americans," Seattle Times, Aug. 13, 1981, p. B1.
3. Sue Chin, "A United Voice in Community," International Examiner, Feb. 20, 1985.

Part 10/The District Comes of Age

1. Much of the material on Redress was taken from Calvin Naito and Esther Scott case study entitled "Against All Odds: The Japanese Americans' Campaign for Redress," Case Program, John F. Kennedy School of Government, Harvard University, 1990.

Selected Bibliography

Gudrun Anderson. *Three Generations of Chinese Family which Figures in Queer Story of Wealth and Oriental Tradition,* Seattle Post-Intelligencer, September 23, 1917.

Kurt E. Armbruster. Orphan Road: The Railroad Comes to Seattle 1853-1911, Washington State University Press, Pullman, 1999.

Peter Bacho. Dark Blue Suit and Other Stories, University of Washington Press, Seattle, 1997.

Clarence B. Bagley. *The Anti-Chinese Agitation and Riots,* in History of Seattle, Volume II, Clarke Publisher, Chicago, 1916, pages 455-473.

Richard C. Berner. Seattle 1900-1920: From Boomtown Urban, Turbulence to Restoration, Charles Press, Seattle, 1991.

Richard C. Berner. Seattle 1921-1940: From Boom to Bust, Charles Press, Seattle,1992.

Carlos Bulosan. America is in the Heart, University of Washington Press, 1973.

Sucheng Chan. Asian Americans: An Interpretive History, Twayne Publishers, Boston, 1991.

Jack Chen. The Chinese of America, Harper and Row, San Francisco, 1980.

Ron Chew, editor. Reflections of Seattle's Chinese Americans: The First 100 Years, University of Washington Press/Wing Luke Asian Museum, Seattle, 1994.

Art Chin. Golden Tassels: A History of the Chinese in Washington 1857 -1977, Art Chin, Seattle, 1987.

Doug Chin and Art Chin. Uphill: The Settlement and Diffusion of Chinese in Seattle Washington, Shorey Books, Seattle, 1974.

Doug Chin and Peter Bacho. *The International District: History of an Urban, Ethnic Neighborhood in Seattle,* International Examiner, 1984.

Sue Chin, '*A united voice in community,*' International Examiner, February 20, 1985.

Fred Cordova. Filipinos: Forgotten Asian Americans, Demonstration Project for Asian Americans, Seattle, 1983.

Paul de Barros. Jackson Street after Dark: The Roots of Jazz in Seattle, Sasquatch Books, Seattle, 1993.
Florangela Davila. *The Struggle for the Soul of Seattle's International District,* The Seattle Times, October 15, 2000, page 1, 12-13.

Ferdinand M. de Leon. *Carlos Bulosan, in the Heart,* The Seattle Times, August 8, 1999, pages L1-L3.

Ferdinand M. de Leon. *Wing Luke Museum Coming of Age,* June 22, 1997, pages L1-2.

Paul Dorpat. *Seattle's first Chinatown,* The Seattle Times/Seattle Post-Intelligencer Pacific Magazine, November 25, 1990, page 46.

Paul Dorpat. *Seattle's Second School,* The Seattle Times/Seattle Post-Intelligencer Pacific Magazine, June 14, 1992, page 38.

Howard Droker. *Seattle Race Relations during the Second World War,* Pacific Northwest Quarterly, October 1986.

Jim Faber. *Chinese lottery was a chance to 'get well,'* The Seattle Times Magazine, October 27, 1974, page 7.

Chris Friday. *Silent Sojourn: The Chinese Along the Lower Columbia River, 1870-1900,* The Annals of The Chinese Historical Society of the Pacific Northwest 1985-86, pages 30-62.

Carey Quan Gelernier. *Exiled within: Internment forever altered Seattle's Japanese-American community,* The Seattle Times/Seattle Post-Intelligencer, February 16, 1992, pages 1, 10-11.

Donald Guimary and Jack Masson. *The Exploitation of Chinese Labor in Alaska Salmon Industry,* Chinese America: History and Perspectives 1990, pages 91-106.

Kazuro Ito. Issei: A History of Japanese Immigrants in North America, Seattle, Executive Committee for Publication of Issei, 1973.

S.K. Kanda. *The Japanese in Washington,* Washington Magazine, 1908, pages 193-197.

George Kinnear. Anti-Chinese Riots at Seattle Washington, Feb. 8, 1886, Seattle, Wash., Feb. 8, 1911.

Alan Chong Lau. Blues and Greens: A Produce Worker's Journal, University of Hawaii Press, Honolulu, 2000.

Rose Hum Lee. The Chinese in the United States, Hong Kong University Press, Hong Kong, 1960.

Stanford M. Lyman. Chinese Americans, Random House, New York, 1974.

Ronald E. Magden. Furusato: Tacoma-Pierce County Japanese 1888-1977, A Project of Nikkeijinkae: Tacoma Japanese Community Service, Tacoma, 1998.

Diane Mei Mark and Ginger Chih. A Place Called Chinese America, Dubuque, Kendall/Hunt Publishing, 1982.

Ruthanne Lum McCunn. Chinese American Portraits, University of Washington Press, Seattle, 1996.

Lucille McDonald. *The First Chinese Resident in Seattle*, The Seattle Times Sunday Magazine, September 11, 1955.

S. Frank Miyamoto. *Social Solidarity Among the Japanese in Seattle*, University of Washington Publication in Social Sciences, December 1939.

S. Frank Miyamoto. *An Immigrant Community in America*, in East Across the Pacific edited by Hilary Conroy and T. Scott Miyakawa, CLIO Press, Santa Barbara, 1972, pages 217-243.

S. Frank Miyamoto and Robert W. O'Brien. *A Survey of Some Changes in the Seattle Japanese Communitysince Evacuation*, in Research Studies of the State College of Washington, June 1947, pages 147-154.

Murray Morgan. Skid Road: An Informal Portrait of Seattle, University of Washington Press, Seattle, 1982.

Calvin Naito and Esther Scott. *Against All Odds: The Japanese Americans' Campaign for Redress*, Case Program, John F. Kennedy School of Government, Harvard University, 1990.

Gail M. Nomura. *Washington's Asian/Pacific American Communities*, in Peoples of Washington: Perspectives on Cultural Diversity, Sid White and S.E. Solberg editors, Washington State University Press, 1989.

John Okada. No-No Boy, University of Washington Press, Seattle, 1979.

Elizabeth Rhodes. *Ruby Chow,* The Seattle Times/Seattle Post-Intelligencer Pacific Magazine, December 9, 1984.

Larry Roberts. *Kingdome: Fears of traffic jams, loss of city revenues, business dislocation, sidewalk collapse,* The Seattle Sun, March 3, 1976, page 1.

Roger Sale. Seattle Past to Present, University of Washington Press, Seattle, 1976.

C.F. Schmid, C.E. Nobbe, and A.E. Mitchell. Nonwhite Races: State of Washington, Washington State Planning and Community Affairs Agency, Olympia, 1968.

Carlos A. Schwantes. *Unemployment, Disinheritance, and the Origins of Labor Militancy in the Pacific Northwest, 1885-86*, in Experiences in the Promise Land: Essays in Pacific Northwest History, University of Washington Press, 1986, pages 179-194.

Susan Schwartz. *Chinatown Walk: History, culture - more than just restaurants*, The Seattle Times, May 1, 1976, page B1.

Susan Schwartz. *International District stirs after 'nap,'* The Seattle Times, February 8, 1976, pages A26-27.

John C. Shideler. Coal Towns in the Cascades: A Centennial History of Roslyn and Cle Elum, Washington, Melior Publications, Spokane, 1986.

David Suffia. *Asian Still Fear Stadium Impact, Residents feel they've been misled,* The Seattle Times, November 17, 1972, page A13.

Ronald Takaki. Strangers from a Different Shore: A History of Asian Americans, Penguin Books, New York, 1989.

David Takami. A History of Japanese Americans in Seattle, University of Washington Press/Wing Luke Asian Museum, Seattle, 1998.

David Takami. *Executive Order 9066: 50 years Before and 50 Years After*, Wing Luke Asian Museum, 1992.

David Takami. *Shared Dreams: A History of Asians and Pacific Americans in Washington State*, Washington State Centennial Commission, 1989.

Tokichi Tanaka. *The Japanese in Seattle*, Coast Magazine, November, 1909, pages 249-258.

William Wilcox. *Anti-Chinese Riots in Washington*, Washington Historical Quarterly, Vol. XX, Number 3, July 1929, pages 204-212.

Robert Edward Wynne. Reaction to the Chinese in the Pacific Northwest and British Columbia, 1850 to 1910, Arno Press, Inc., 1978.

Paul Yee. Saltwater City: An Illustrated History of the Chinese in Vancouver, University of Washington Press, Seattle, 1988.

Helen Zia. Asian American Dreams: The Emergence of an Asian American People; Farrar, Straw and Girous, New York, 2000.

Index

Hing Hay Park. International Examiner file photo.

International Examiner

The International Examiner is a 501(c)3 non-profit corporation. It is the oldest and the only non-profit pan-Asian American newspaper in the United States. The Examiner also publishes the Pacific Reader, the only Asian American review of books in the country. The International Examiner press is devoted to publishing works by and about Asian Americans in the Pacific Northwest.